Yale University
SEES/YCIAS Outreach
Box 13A
New Have

BARBARA SILBERDICK FEINBERG

MARX AND MARXISM

FRANKLIN WATTS
NEW YORK ■ LONDON ■ TORONTO ■ SYDNEY ■ 1985
AN IMPACT BOOK

THIS BOOK IS DEDICATED TO THE MEMORY OF MY PARENTS, HARRIET AND NORMAN SILBERDICK.

Library of Congress Cataloging in Publication Data
Feinberg, Barbara Silberdick.
Marx and Marxism.
(An Impact book)
Bibliography: p.
Summary: Recounts the life of the nineteenth-century German philosopher and interprets his ideas, which played a revolutionary role in the development of Communism.
1. Marx, Karl, 1818–1883—Juvenile literature.
2. Philosophers—Germany—Biography—Juvenile literature.
3. Communism—Juvenile literature. [1. Marx, Karl, 1818–1883] 2. Philosophers. 3. Communism] I. Title.
HX39.5.F385 1985   335.4′092′4 [B] [92]   85-11474
ISBN 0-531-10065-0

Copyright © 1985 by Barbara Silberdick Feinberg
All rights reserved
Printed in the United States of America
5 4 3

CONTENTS

Introduction
The Man and the Theory
1

PART ONE
KARL MARX, THE MAN
7

Chapter One
The Young Marx
9

Chapter Two
Marx Abroad
22

Chapter Three
Marx in Revolt
34

Chapter Four
Marx in Exile
47

PART TWO
MARXISM, THE THEORY
59

Chapter Five
History as a Science
61

Chapter Six
Workers as Victims
72

Chapter Seven
Revolution as a Solution
83

Chapter Eight
A Vision of the Future
94

Chapter Nine
Marxism After Marx
105

Further Reading
119

Index
120

MARX
AND
MARXISM

I am most grateful to my husband, Gary, for his encouragement and support. Not only did he teach me to use our microcomputer so that this book could be prepared by means of word processing, he also made it possible for me to secure much needed research materials.

I would like to express my thanks to my sons Jeremy and Douglas for being willing to share computer time with their mother.

I owe a special debt to Mrs. Nathaniel Williams, who admonished me to stop talking about doing this project someday and to get to work writing it out instead. In the absence of Mrs. Williams' prompting, the book might never have been written.

INTRODUCTION
THE MAN AND THE THEORY

During the twentieth century, two different political systems, Western democracy and communism, have been competing for the loyalty of the world's peoples. Most Western democracies have economies based on private enterprise, but communist nations rely on state-run and -planned economies. While Western democracy values the dignity and worth of each individual, communism stresses the importance of common ties to a group. Although Western democracies are tolerant of many different religious and political beliefs, their communist counterparts frown upon the exercise of religion and require their citizens to submit to one political viewpoint.

The political viewpoint that modern communist societies prescribe for their citizens is based on the doctrines of Karl Marx, a nineteenth-century European philosopher. He rejected the notions of Western democracy, believing they promoted selfishness and competition among people as well as the tyranny of powerful employers over their weak employees. In his writings,

Marx sought to explain why the workers of his day and age labored long and hard for miserable wages under terrible conditions. He blamed their mistreatment on the economic system of private enterprise. Marx predicted that because the workers would not endure their misfortunes forever, they would inevitably wage a revolution to free themselves from oppression. Then the tyranny of the powerful over the weak would come to an end. Marx even went so far as to sketch out a vague vision of the future in which all humankind would live in harmony and prosperity as equals.

Today, over a third of the population of the world considers itself to be Marxist. Nations on the continents of Europe, Asia, Africa, and South America claim to accept Marx's criticism of Western democracies, his advocacy of workers' revolutions, and his description of a future society. However, Marxism has undergone many changes since Marx first wrote down his ideas. By studying what he said and the way his immediate successors interpreted his ideas, it should be possible to gain a better understanding of the origins of modern communism. Modern communism claims to be a Marxist doctrine, but some have argued that it has strayed from its Marxist roots. After reading Marx's views, the reader will be able to decide for himself or herself how valid that argument is.

This book is divided into two parts. The first section offers a brief description of the life and times of Karl Marx. This is intended to provide a framework, or context, for Marx's ideas, to explain how these ideas developed, and to perhaps suggest why Marx may have reached the conclusions he did. The second part presents Marx's ideas and shows their strengths and weaknesses. It also looks at some of the ways Marx's thought was interpreted after his death when the conditions he had described changed. With this background, readers should be able to have a better understanding of what Marxism actually is.

The study of Karl Marx's life and thought is filled with ironies; that is, what happened to him and to his ideas often turned out differently from or opposite to what might have been expected. Marx, who devoted himself to the plight of laboring men, women, and children, never worked in a factory a day in his life. In fact, he rarely held a job for any length of time. At the time he wrote his most famous works, the *Communist Manifesto* and *Capital*, this son of a prosperous German family was a threadbare refugee in a strange country, barely managing to support his wife and children on his meager earnings as a sometime newspaperman. Mostly he could be found in the reading room of the British Museum working on his studies of history and economy. To make ends meet, he often depended on the generosity of his friend, Friedrich Engels. Engels was a partner in his family's textile business. In effect, Marx was supported by the labor of workers whose lives he hoped to change.

Marx was a devoted family man, proud of his wife's aristocratic background, and quite willing to enjoy life's pleasures and comforts. How ironic it was that in his writings, he heaped abuse on families, claiming they were held together merely by economic ties, not by bonds of affection. He also condemned aristocrats for leading useless lives. He criticized a life of pleasure and comfort because in his day, such a life was available to only a few while the many worked hard and had little to show for their efforts.

It is also ironic that during all the social and political upheavals of nineteenth-century Europe, Marx, the author of revolutionary tracts, chose to write rather than to fight. Yet, even as a writer, Marx found that these were dangerous and exciting times to be alive. In an age of government censorship of political opinions, Marx's articles and books were deemed perhaps more dangerous than bullets or guns. Weapons could indeed kill, but thoughts could encourage and perpetuate unrest and dissatisfaction beyond the lifetime of any rebellious citizen. So government officials examined and frequently restricted what could appear in print. As Marx published his thoughts and beliefs, he came into constant conflict with the authorities whose censorship he protested or defied. These officials forced him into exile from one nation to another so that he became the proverbial "man without a country." The life of a philosopher, of a scholar, is quite often seen as uneventful and dull, but Karl Marx's career was anything but quiet and calm.

A study of Marx's thought yields perhaps as many ironies as the study of Marx's life. His nineteenth-century writings have had an enormous impact on twentieth-century governments and peoples. However, Marx's particular impact may not have been quite what he intended. For example, he addressed his ideas to the workers of industrially advanced states in Europe. Yet, today, the people who seem most attracted to Marx's doctrines are not workers, but peasants who live in industrially underdeveloped societies. To them, Marxism represents a hope for the future, an escape from poverty and degradation. These people are certainly not the audience Marx had in mind. To others, including the descendents of the Western European workers whose lives Marx did seek to change, Marxism is often seen as a menace, a threat to their social, economic, and political systems.

Marx presented his ideas in the form of a theory, a set of hypotheses explaining the way people or objects behave under certain circumstances. Theory also makes predictions about the way people or objects will behave when conditions are changed. However, it is as an ideology, a simplified set of ideas and slogans, that Marxism has had its greatest impact on the peoples of this world. It is as the author of that ideology that Marx is remembered today.

This transformation is ironic because Marx condemned ideologies. He described them as justifications for the way things were, as rationalizations of the *status quo*. He saw ideologies as the way people in power excused or disguised their misdeeds and misrule. While some scholars today view ideologies as a means of inciting people to action, Marx saw ideologies as a means of keeping people quiet and complacent. For example, he argued that governments of his day might proclaim themselves to be democracies even though they were not democracies. They did this to mislead people into believing that the people ruled themselves. Marx insisted that in fact the right to vote was restricted to a small percentage of the population and the real power to make decisions was held by cabinet ministers and not the people's representatives! These governments lied to their citizens in order to keep themselves in power. It is even more ironic that by using ideology in the same way that Marx condemned, Marxist governments today mislead people into believing that they are truly democratic.

Marxism as Marx wrote it was a complicated descriptive theory rather than a simplified ideology. That theory certainly sparked controversy both during Marx's lifetime and afterward. People were not always certain that Marx meant what he said or said what he meant. Some of his ideas were not entirely clear to his readers. For example, when he urged workers to seize power, did he mean that they should use force and violence to set up a new government or that they should go to the polls in large numbers and vote in a new government? This is why his theory has been subject to so many different interpretations.

There is another reason why Marx's theory has been reinterpreted again and again. The conditions he originally described changed so things did not happen the way he predicted they would, a truly ironic situation for Marx and his followers. Instead of the economic collapse and confusion he predicted, there was growth and expansion. Instead of workers' lives becoming more and more miserable, their wages rose and they became better off. Instead of the rise of a unified international movement of workers, there were constant disagreements and disunity among workers as their patriotic and nationalistic feelings grew stronger. Instead of the world revolution of workers he urged and expected, there was world war among nations, with workers fighting one another.

After Marx's death, his followers engaged in lengthy debates over the meanings of his ideas and how best to apply them. These discussions took up much of the period from the 1880s to the outbreak of World War I, in 1914. By that time, it began to look as if Marx's ideas had become obsolete. It looked as though his writings would be left to the pages of history books. However, in 1917, the greatest irony of all occurred. The Soviet regime came to power in Russia and transformed Marxism for all time into a system of beliefs imposed and enforced by brutal governmental power. Before the Russian Revolution, Marxism had been a system of beliefs for those who lacked power!

As has been shown, in Marx's career as well as in his writings, what might have been expected to happen rarely seemed to happen. To see what did happen, it is useful to take a closer look at Marx's life. This section of the book is divided into four periods: Marx's youth, his years abroad, his adventures as a reluctant revolutionary, and his experiences as a refugee in Great Britain.

PART ONE

KARL MARX

THE MAN

CHAPTER ONE
THE
YOUNG MARX

Germany, the land of Karl Marx's birth, was made up of a series of small kingdoms and states, loosely joined together in the German Confederation. From 1815 to 1819, reform movements arose seeking to draw educated classes closer to their rulers and to give the Germans a sense of national identity. In Prussia, the German state where the Marx family lived, those demands for reform included the creation of a constitutional government, to limit what government could legally do, and an elected legislature to represent the people. By 1819, Austria's Count Metternich (1773–1859) was able to convince the members of the German Confederation that the reformers were seeking to overthrow the established order. The Federal Diet of the Confederation, a legislative body, responded to his warnings by issuing the repressive Carlsbad Decrees. These decrees introduced censorship and disbanded student patriotic societies that had spearheaded the reform movements.

It was into this world of reform and repression that Karl Marx was born on May 5, 1818. His father, Heinrich, was a lawyer who enjoyed reading about philosophy and history. He accepted the ideas of the French Enlightenment: the belief in reason, in the possibility of man's perfection, in the importance of freedom. He was interested in the reform movements of the day and wanted Prussia to become a strong constitutional state. Karl's mother, Henrietta, had been born in Holland and never became truly fluent in German. She was fairly wealthy, and although Marx later looked to her for financial help, he never developed close ties with her.

Both parents were Jewish, and there were many rabbis in the Marx family tree, but Heinrich Marx converted to Protestantism before Karl was born. Jews could not serve in government positions or practice certain professions, such as law, unless they became Christians. When he was six, Karl was baptized as a Christian, because Jews were not permitted to attend public schools. The alternative schooling was decidedly inferior. In view of the practical reasons for his father's conversion, it is unlikely that organized religion played an important role in the Marx family's lives. Heinrich Marx never denied his Jewish origins, but Karl Marx became ashamed of his background.

Marx was the third of nine children, but as a youngster he never drew close to any of his brothers and sisters. He did enjoy bullying them. Since they were sickly and intellectually slow, it was easy for Karl to dominate them. His father soon became aware that Karl was arrogant, demanding, and self-centered. Furthermore, he perceived that his child was driven by an inner passion: what Karl did, he did to excess. This troubled Heinrich Marx. However, he did little to curb his son's temperament. He even indulged his son's whims probably because he considered Karl the most intelligent of his brood. He was certain that Karl would make something of himself.

Karl spent his early years in the city of Trier, where he had been born. It was a city of churches and vineyards. It was nonindustrial and traditional. Most of its population was terribly poor. Karl Marx developed a sensitivity to the different lifestyles of the well-to-do and the poor very early in life. Fortunately for him, his childhood was spent as a member of the more privileged class.

The city was part of Prussia but located quite close to the French border. It had been under French rule from 1795 to 1815 so the ideas of the French Enlightenment accepted by Heinrich Marx were familiar and almost commonplace to other citizens of Trier. Karl Marx developed pro–French sympathies by growing up in this French-German Rhineland city and by listening to his father's discussions of the principles of the Enlightenment. However, Heinrich Marx believed in obedience to the government of Prussia, a loyalty his son was firmly to reject.

From 1830 to 1835, Karl attended the Friedrich Wilhelm gymnasium, a cross between the American secondary school and junior college, in order to prepare for university studies. His father had intended him to have a professional career. The school was not elitist since many of the students were sons of poor peasants and artisans preparing for the priesthood. Discipline was somewhat relaxed in that the school encouraged a spirit of free inquiry among the students, or at least a critical attitude toward the Prussian government.

Marx's life at the school was full of excitement and suspense. Prussian officials suspected that the teachers and pupils at Marx's school endorsed liberal beliefs, such as Marx's father had, that Prussia should be governed by a constitution limiting the powers of the king and guaranteeing the citizens rights protected by law. As a result the school was constantly under police surveillance. For Marx it was a firsthand experience of how a repressive government could use its power to protect its self-interest, to prevent needed reforms from occurring. Marx could not fail to be aware that the government of King Frederick William III (1770–1840) was actively suppressing liberal reformist uprisings in Prussia lest they become revolutions like those which were sweeping through the rest of Europe in the 1830s. Perhaps Marx's concern with injustice had its roots in his school experiences in Trier.

Marx made no lasting friendships at the school nor did he live up to his father's expectations of academic success. He did excel in German and Latin composition, but his grades in history, religion, French translation, physics, and Greek were only adequate or mediocre. Reports of his conduct toward fellow students and teachers were good. However, unlike his father, his teachers did not see him as particularly outstanding or possessed by an inner drive to achieve.

In order to graduate, Karl had to submit a series of essays to the faculty of his school. One is particularly interesting, "Reflections of a Young Man on Choosing an Occupation." In it, he proclaimed that the greatest men in history were not those who worked for themselves to gain fame or material success but were those who sacrificed themselves for mankind! In this essay lay the seeds of Karl Marx's future—although at the time it was doubtful that he himself knew it.

From 1835 to 1836, Marx was sent to the University of Bonn, a small university noted for its brilliant faculty. This was quite a change for Marx because Bonn was a Prussian city about four times larger than Trier. The atmosphere was gay and exciting, especially enticing to students who wished to pursue an active social life. Since Marx was freed at last from the immediate supervision of his family, he was determined to enjoy himself. He took courses in poetry, art, and law, and his teachers considered him "diligent and attentive," but, no matter how seriously he plunged into his studies, they did not seem to take up all of his time. His interests lay elsewhere, as his constant demands for money from home suggested. Marx was preoccupied with having a good time, often going to drinking parties, such as those later immortalized in operettas like *The Student Prince*. To the disgust of his father, Marx was actually arrested for being drunk and disorderly and spent a day in jail. Having a good time also meant dueling, an activity designed to prove one's courage and masculinity. So Marx fought a duel. His parents were constantly worried about the state of his health as well as his behavior and his debts because he tended to burn the candle at both ends, each end to excess.

An important student pastime was club memberships. These should not be compared to modern fraternities, but in some ways they served the same social functions of distinguishing "insiders" from "outsiders" and bringing their members together in bonds of fellowship. They often served political functions as well. Since there was no constitution and no way in which political criticisms could be legally voiced, student clubs became an important avenue of opposition. To fulfill his social needs, Marx joined a tavern club, made up of middle-class students. The more aristocratic university students had their own exclusive organizations. The two sets of associations were often in conflict.

Since Marx had dreams of becoming a poet, he also joined a poet's club. The club had strong political overtones. Some of its members were known as political activists. University students sought to achieve liberal reforms by creating disturbances and riots, as well as through discussions and debates, a phenomenon the 1830s had in common with the 1960s in America. In

1833, a group of these students had even attempted to disrupt a meeting of the Federal Diet of the German Confederation, sitting in Frankfurt, in order to overthrow the monarchy and proclaim a German republic. While Marx was a student at Bonn, a number of these politically active students were expelled from the university. Others were arrested. It was a heady atmosphere, charged with political debate and risk of imprisonment.

Given Marx's drinking bouts, duels, debts, and political entanglements, it is not surprising that his father transferred him to the University of Berlin in 1836. In contrast to the University of Bonn, the University of Berlin demanded hard work from its students and was intolerant of political activism or wild student escapades. It was located in the capital city of Prussia, noted for its disciplined, industrious citizens.

As was expected of him, Marx plunged into work. He concentrated on studying law, history, and philosophy, but his studies were basically undirected, that is, no one told him what to do or when to do it. For example, Marx chose his own reading assignments, taking lengthy and detailed notes, and did translations from Latin into German on his own. He also started to learn the Italian and English languages. Students in Marx's day were not required to attend as many classes as they do today. They were expected to plan and carry out their own studies while occasionally attending lectures offered by professors.

Now Heinrich Marx became concerned that his son was working far too hard and proceeded to write him long letters filled with instructions about moderating his work habits, but the advice was ignored. Marx neglected all social obligations, including visits to three of his father's former colleagues who were now judges. Until 1838, when he died, Heinrich Marx wrote letters pleading with his son to make something of himself. He accused his son of obsessiveness, the tendency to get involved to excess; selfishness; sloppiness; indifference to the family; and a tendency to waste money. Heinrich Marx blamed himself for indulging his son at the same time that he urged him to take responsibility for himself, in other words, to grow up!

Marx felt burdened by his father's demands that he settle upon a career and live up to his father's expectations of success. At the same time, his father was urging him not to drive himself so hard, but from young Marx's point of view, it was necessary to work hard in order to gain the learning necessary to a successful career. What's more, he wasn't sure what career he wanted.

Marx still had notions of becoming a poet, much to the disappointment of his father. He had been writing poems and sending them home, but his father urged him to write something longer that would bring him public acclaim. His father was willing to concede that the son might become a writer, but not a poet, at best an uncertain career. In 1841, two of Marx's poems were actually published, but in the meantime he switched from poetry to playwriting in an attempt to placate his father and still be able to pursue his literary interests. He wanted to write a tragic drama, but his father cautioned him to try something more modest instead.

At this point, in the spring of 1837, Marx began to suffer from fatigue and nervous exhaustion. The pressure to live up to his father's expectations and to pursue his own interests had led him to study day and night. This regimen took its toll on his health. Upon the advice of a doctor, Marx left Berlin and moved to a nearby fishing village from April to the following autumn. He spent his time reading philosophy and walking around the countryside. Then he felt well enough to resume his studies.

While he returned to his self-imposed load of heavy reading, Marx found time to extend his literary and philosophical interests. He joined the Young Hegelians, followers of the ideas of the philosopher Georg Hegel (1770–1831), who until his death had been a leading professor at the University of Berlin. Hegel had originated a theory which, from Marx's point of view, glorified the institution of the state. Marx had little loyalty to the repressive Prussian state while Hegel appeared to hold it in very high regard.

Hegel claimed that history was moving in the direction of greater freedom for humankind and that at any point in time, the state represented the degree of freedom humankind was capable of achieving. Hegel had been a loyal supporter of the autocratic Prussian state, since from his point of view, it represented the best possible political organization for his day and age. Accordingly, he won the admiration and respect of the Prussian government. However, his theories suggested that as history progressed, the Prussian autocracy would be replaced by a new and superior form of government, granting more freedom to its citizens.

It was this latter notion that appealed to Marx and to the Young Hegelians. Because the Young Hegelians were concerned with historical change, Prussian authorities considered them to be a dangerous group of subversives, seeking to undermine beliefs in the existing order. Despite his dislike for Hegel's ideas of the state, Marx did prefer studying ideas to studying facts, and he was attracted to the students' opposition to the existing Prussian government. So he reluctantly joined this movement. While he rejected Hegel's views of the Prussian state, what he learned about Hegel's method of analysis of historical change would have a profound influence on his own interpretation of history at a later point in his life.

Marx became a member of the Doctor's Club, a political and philosophical offshoot of the Young Hegelian movement. The club idolized Bruno Bauer (1809–1882), a theologian who regarded the Scriptures as mythology rather than history. For Bauer, biblical personages were fictional characters, not real ones. He claimed that the Bible was a product of people's imagination based on their need to understand the unknown. Marx was known to have attended Bauer's lectures.

Perhaps it was Bauer's influence that led the Young Hegelians to consider abandoning their religious beliefs. It is claimed that Marx had renounced his religion at the age of sixteen. Since his family was only nominally Protestant, this was not a difficult thing for him to do. Karl Marx remained a lifelong atheist, that is, a person who does not believe in the existence of a deity. In his mature writings, Marx would have a lot to say about the role religion played in people's lives; none of it was particularly flattering.

Under the influence of the Young Hegelians, Marx's interest in philosophy intensified. Bauer urged him to get a doctoral degree so that he would be qualified to teach at the university level. In 1838, the year of his father's death, Marx began to work on his doctoral dissertation, "The Difference between Democritean and Epicurean Philosophy of Nature." With his usual ability to immerse himself in subjects that captured his interest, Marx threw himself into studies of these ancient Greek philosophies. He finally completed his thesis in 1841. The completed work demonstrated Marx's capacity for critical analysis, an ability that would characterize most of his later writings. It might even be said that Marx was much better at tearing subject matter apart and finding fault with others' ideas than he was at putting things together and providing constructive solutions.

At Bauer's suggestion, Marx decided to submit his thesis to the University of Jena, a small university located in the Grand Duchy of Saxe-Weimar, outside Prussian jurisdiction. Marx had chosen not to take his degree at the University of Berlin because the academic standards at the University of Jena were considered more lax. More important, Marx was aware that the University of Berlin had undergone administrative changes which placed in control officials and faculty hostile to the Young Hegelians. By 1841 the Young Hegelians had drifted toward republicanism, elective government without a monarch, and had questioned the aristocratic social system of the Prussian state. University officials and Prussian authorities feared that they might take action to put their antimonarchical, antiaristocratic ideas into effect. Marx received his degree from the University of Jena in April 1841.

Once he had become a doctor of philosophy, Marx intended to join Bauer on the faculty of the University of Bonn, where Bauer was teaching after having been transferred from his post at the University of Berlin. However, Marx did not receive an appointment to the faculty, and he found it difficult to obtain a teaching post anywhere because his ties to Bauer and the Young Hegelians were offensive to university officials. The devout King of Prussia, Frederick William IV (1795–1861), had objected so strongly to Bauer's interpretation of Christianity that he had personally commanded that Bauer be removed from his position and barred from teaching elsewhere in Prussia. The Young Hegelians were already under suspicion for their political views.

In 1841, the Prussian government issued a new censorship decree allowing censors to bar from publication any writings offensive to religion, morality, or goodwill. This so provoked Marx that he wrote an essay attacking the decree as ineffectual. He argued that secrecy stirred even more interest in banned items than publishing them would. He held that a free press could inform people. From Marx's point of view, the effect of the decree was to make incompetent censors into judges of trained and informed writers. The article was published by Arnold Ruge in a liberal journal in Switzerland, the German censors having banned publication of the article in Prussia.

His article on censorship was attacked by the *Kolnische Zeitung (Cologne Times)*. In defense of his position, Marx submitted an article to the *Rheinische Zeitung (Rhine Times)*, a rival newspaper somewhat more liberal in its orientation. Having tried his hand at journalism, Marx began to write more articles for *Rheinische Zeitung*. Marx was not a neutral observer of events. The articles he wrote were indeed inflammatory and accusatory. His writing resembled some modern investigative reporting, but Marx was less concerned with the facts than with the corruption and injustice they revealed. He took up residence in Cologne, the most progressive industrial city in Prussia, to continue his newspaper writing. Journalism was one career still open to him, and it was the only career he would ever pursue.

Since the *Rheinische Zeitung* lacked strong leadership, he recommended that his Young Hegelian friend, journalist Adolf Rutenberg, become editor of the newspaper. However, Marx soon realized that Rutenberg was incompetent and was using the paper solely as a platform for Young Hegelian rhetoric. At this stage of his life, Marx was becoming disenchanted with the Young Hegelians. To him, they were more interested in publicity seeking than in genuine issues of injustice and reform. When Prussian authorities, suspicious of the Young Hegelian ramblings Rutenberg published, caused him to be ousted as editor, Marx replaced him in October 1842, at the age of twenty-four. The Young Hegelians had expected Marx to come to Rutenberg's defense and were disappointed in him. In turn, Marx broke away from them and as editor of the newspaper, he began to promote reforms rather than to air Young Hegelian ideas.

Upon assuming the editorship, Marx had had to promise Prussian authorities not to express any sentiments favoring France, Prussia's traditional enemy, and to show how progressive Prussia was becoming; however, Marx began to question the policies of the Prussian government in print. His writings covered a range of social and economic problems of the day, including the issue of outrageous laws against the theft of dead timber wood by peasants, who had traditionally used the stolen wood for fuel, and the closing of a Leipzig newspaper as a result of censorship. These kinds of articles not only reflected Marx's opinions, they attracted more readers. Under Marx's editorship, the newspaper's circulation increased impressively.

However, when the *Rheinische Zeitung* published an article critical of the czarist regime in Russia, Prussia's chief European ally, the King of Prussia gave in to Russian pressure and on January 21, 1843, ordered the newspaper closed by March 31. In the interim, the paper was censored even more closely prior to the publication of each issue. On March 17, Marx resigned, feeling that he could accomplish little of any use.

Karl Marx had lost his first job, but he soon gained a wife. On June 19, 1843, he married Jenny von Westphalen, an aristocratic young woman four years his senior. Theirs was a love match. Karl and Jenny had met when he was a schoolboy in Trier; her brother Edgar was one of Marx's classmates, and Marx's older sister, Sophie, was Jenny's close friend. Karl admired Jenny's father, Ludwig, for his learning and culture. Ludwig von Westphalen was a Prussian state official, related on his mother's side to Scottish nobility. Marx and the elder von Westphalen enjoyed reciting Shakespeare to each other. Marx even came to prefer Jenny's father's company and advice to that of his own father. He went so far as to dedicate his doctoral thesis to Ludwig von Westphalen.

Jenny was a very pretty woman with a perfectly oval face, green eyes, and auburn hair. Marx had once described her as the "Queen of the Ball." She had been attracted to this intense, dark-haired young man with deep, defiant eyes. Their courtship had been long and stormy. They had become secretly engaged to marry when Karl left to study at the University of Bonn, but their courtship was conducted mostly by letter, for Karl rarely returned home. Even then, correspondence between them was sporadic. Karl was not a frequent letter writer, and it was not considered proper for a young lady to write to her suitor unless she was formally engaged.

After a year at Bonn, Karl admitted his feelings about Jenny to his father, who then became an intermediary in their off-again, on-again relationship. When doubts, jealousies, and fears interrupted the progress of the courtship, Heinrich Marx had to soothe ruffled feelings. One of the reasons he had pressed his son to settle down and choose a career was his concern over Karl's ability to support an aristocratic wife like Jenny. He also questioned the depth of his son's feelings, given Karl's intense, but sometimes short-lived, enthusiasms. While Karl won his father over to their side, Jenny persuaded her father to consent to the wedding, but by the time the marriage finally took place, both fathers had died. Other members of both families remained firm in their opposition to the match. Issues such as the differences in background and ages kept the two families from accepting the marriage. No members of the Marx family came to the wedding, and only Jenny's mother and brother attended her at the ceremony. The couple honeymooned in Switzerland.

As Marx's youth drew to a close, he had settled on a career and he had chosen a wife. He had developed a concern for the underprivileged and a deep hostility toward the Prussian state. He had been trained as a philosopher and had learned to question what he read or saw. He was a passionate man, capable of prodigious amounts of work but only on subjects that interested him. He had disavowed organized religion, his former political associates, and even his family. He was ready for a new life.

CHAPTER TWO
MARX ABROAD

Paris in 1843 was an exciting and stimulating place, the seat of government of the July Monarchy (1830–1848), a constitutional government in which the upper middle classes exercised power. The right to vote was still restricted, but at least the wealthy could vote for their leaders. Under King Louis-Philippe (1773–1850) and his premier François Guizot (1787–1874), France prospered. In this relatively permissive atmosphere, Paris became a haven for refugees, for left-wing movements, for unpopular causes.

When the Prussian authorities shut down the *Rheinische Zeitung*, Marx and his friend Arnold Ruge, an editor and journalist, had made plans to publish the *Deutsch-Franzosische Jahrbucher (German-French Yearbooks)*, a political review. Since Ruge had moved from Switzerland to Paris, Karl and Jenny planned to join him there. After their honeymoon trip, they had spent the summer of 1843 in Kreuznach at the home of Jenny's mother, where Marx prepared two essays to be published in the *Yearbooks*. One of these was a highly anti-Semitic piece called "On the Jewish Question," the other, the philosophical "Contribution to the Critique of Hegel's Philosophy of Law," demonstrating how much further he had moved from the Young Hegelian circle. The latter was printed in 1844 in the only edition of the yearbook ever to be published.

At the end of October 1843, Karl Marx and his bride scraped enough funds together to travel to Paris. Having grown up in Trier, Marx had always had a fondness for all things French. For him, life in Paris was to be a change from the drab restrictions of Prussia. There was the excitement of new ideas and new friendships. Marx received introductions to people from all walks of life. He met a number of famous Parisians at the Countess d'Agoult's salon and enjoyed mingling with the literary and artistic celebrities of the day. He happily circulated among the upper classes of French society and certainly took pleasure in sharing the comforts and luxuries of their lifestyle.

At the other end of the social spectrum, he became acquainted with French and German workingmen. He began to attend the meetings of German artisans' secret societies. He found their political ideas crude but admired their sense of brotherhood, of solidarity. His interest in them, in the quality of their lives, in the economic role they played in society would become a central feature of his theories.

He made it a point to get to know some of the leading radical socialist thinkers of the age. Radicals were people who urged fundamental changes in society or politics and were rarely willing to compromise. Socialists advocated community ownership of factories or industries. Meeting them was an educational as well as a social experience for Marx. He himself was beginning to share some of their views. However, he was more a revolutionary than some of his new acquaintances. Revolutionaries were people who wanted to change society and government completely and all at one time. As a revolutionary, Marx opposed liberal reformers, those who negotiated gradual, piecemeal changes within existing society because they did not go far enough, fast enough. On the other hand, he condemned terrorists who merely preached violence for its own sake and did not concern themselves with the kind of society that would replace the one they were determined to destroy.

He arranged to be introduced to Mikhail Bakunin (1814–1876), a Russian exile who preached terrorism and violence. The two men were to be constantly at odds in the years to come. Marx also held long discussions with Pierre-Joseph Proudhon (1809–1865), a socialist who condemned private property and deplored violence. Proudhon advocated letting local economic organizations take charge. He wanted associations of workers to run the factories. Later, Marx would condemn Proudhon's views as extremely unrealistic and naive.

Most of Marx's friendships were very short-lived because Marx lacked a normal sense of courtesy, of give-and-take. Marx was unwilling to accept views that differed from his own, and a political disagreement always became a personal disagreement. For Marx, the stuff of life was politics, and he took politics all too seriously. In that sense he was quite domineering, rather tyrannical in his relationships with the intellectuals he met. He never forgot and he never forgave.

Thus it was not surprising that Marx and Ruge had a falling out. On the surface, they appeared to disagree about the character of a mutual friend, Georg Herwegh, the poet. Ruge had attacked Herwegh for his luxuriant and perhaps immoral lifestyle; Marx defended the poet. What was really at issue was Ruge's drift toward impractical schemes to reform society, which Marx could not abide. He was a radical and a revolutionary, not a liberal or a reformer. While the two men used their dispute over Herwegh's lifestyle as an excuse to dissolve a friendship, they were really parting company because of their different approaches to social change. Thereafter, Marx used every occasion to slander this former friend. Of course, after he parted with Ruge, their joint publishing venture came to an end and Marx had to find another outlet for his political views. He began to submit articles to a German weekly review called *Vorwarts (Forward)*, founded at one of the Countess d'Agoult's evening parties.

Among the literary friends Marx made at the time was Heinrich Heine (1797–1856), the brilliant German poet. Heine preferred the liberated atmosphere of the July Monarchy to the repressiveness of Prussian life and so had gone into self-imposed exile from his native land. The relationship with Heine was one of the few instances in Marx's life where he proved tolerant of a friend. Marx, the once aspiring poet, deeply admired Heine's poems as well as his satiric attacks on the Prussian government. Yet he recognized that Heine was far from a true revolutionary; that is, Heine wanted changes in the Prussian government but not in society as well. Marx did respect the poet's artistry, however, and Heine, for his part, was a tolerant friend too, for he was willing to endure Marx's endless political harangues. Marx credited Heine with saving the life of his first-born child, a daughter named Jenny. She had had a convulsive attack, and Karl and his wife simply did not know what to do. Desperate and frightened, they stood by helplessly. Just then, Heine came by for a visit. He promptly took the child and bathed her in warm water, stopping the attack.

The one other enduring friendship Marx made during his stay in Paris was with another fellow German, Friedrich Engels. They had met briefly when Marx was the editor of the *Rheinische Zeitung*. At that time, Engels did not wish to get to know Marx any better because he had found Marx to be too arrogant and opinionated. When they met again in Paris, in August 1844, they discovered that they shared common interests and points of view. They both objected to the economic system of the day and wished to replace it with a more radical one. The two men had more in common than politics. In fact, both were intolerant of opposition, witty, blunt to the point of being vulgar, and occasionally coarse.

Friedrich Engels (1820–1895), born in Barmen, a small manufacturing town in the Rhineland of Germany, was the son of a textile manufacturer and was destined to follow in his father's footsteps. Unlike Marx, Engels detested his father but adored his mother. He attended commercial schools and then fulfilled his military obligation to the Prussian state, developing a lifelong interest in military strategy. He disliked the textile business although he returned to it by 1850 when he found he could not make a living as a journalist.

In contrast to Marx, who had no conception of the value of money and spent it freely, Engels was well versed in economics. Engels had other qualities Marx lacked as well. He was a very practical man graced with a good sense of humor. Moreover, he was self-controlled, fluent in many languages, and wrote with ease. Not only in their talents and abilities did the two men complement each other; their lifestyles and appearances revealed contrasts as well. While Marx was the warmhearted family man, Engels remained a womanizing bachelor for the rest of his life. Marx was dark and powerful, while Engels was blond and slender.

It was under Engels' influence that Marx became an acknowledged communist, a socialist who wanted to do away with private property by means of revolution. Engels also was responsible for getting Marx to learn more about economics. The two men decided to collaborate in writing a satire to expose the errors of the Young Hegelians, but Engels soon tired of the project so it was left to Marx to complete the book they referred to between themselves as *The Holy Family*. Published in 1845, it was the first work in which Marx expressed the radical ideas that would become associated with his name.

At the time the two men renewed their acquaintance, in 1844, Jenny had taken the baby for a visit to her mother's home, finding it hard to cope on limited funds with her husband's bohemian lifestyle. Marx meanwhile had been busy writing his "Economic and Philosophical Manuscripts." The manuscripts are important because they contain Marx's early views on the relationship between economy and the state, law, and ethics as well as his preliminary sketches on how people become alienated, feeling separate and apart, from the societies in which they live. These early writings were not published until 1932, when the Moscow Institute of Marxism-Leninism made them available.

Marx also prepared articles for the *Vorwarts* in an attempt to support his family. In the pieces he prepared for *Vorwarts*, his views became increasingly radical. His articles constantly stressed the idea of revolution and advocated the destruction of the old social and political order. This created difficulties with the French censor. When Marx ultimately took up the issue of social reform in Prussia and suggested that a revolution was necessary for any real change to be accomplished there, he found that he had gone too far. The king of Prussia brought pressure to bear on King Louis-Philippe and Francois Guizot to rid Paris of German atheists and revolutionaries. On January 11, 1845, Marx was ordered to leave the country. His life as an exile had begun.

In early February, Marx crossed the border into Belgium and set out for Brussels, where he lived for the next three years. In Brussels, he constantly changed his lodgings, probably to avoid the police as well as his mounting debts. Jenny remained in Paris to sell the furniture and household goods in order to pay for her journey to join her husband. Later that month, the family was reunited. Jenny was ill and pregnant again.

Since Marx had no money with which to live and no job, he borrowed funds from friends, and when all else failed, his friends took up collections for him. For the rest of his life he was to live in this hand-to-mouth fashion. However, Marx did not enjoy being dependent on others for money, and his wounded pride often led him to angry tirades against his fate. When he made an effort to control his temper, Marx tended to suffer ill health. For example, in the summer of 1846, when the family endured further financial reverses, Marx had a severe attack of asthma. As one student of Marx's life has suggested, almost every time the family faced a financial crisis, Marx and Jenny fell ill.

The lot of a refugee in Belgium was not altogether easy in the 1840s. The king of the Belgians, Leopold I (1790–1865), was a native German who assumed the throne of the newly created kingdom when Belgium revolted from Dutch rule in 1830. As the country settled into its new independence, jobs were scarce and outsiders were not made welcome. Every move refugees made was scrutinized by the police. They were allowed to remain in the country only as long as they went about their business and did not become active in the political life of Belgium. If they were found to be involved in politics, they were expelled. That made it hard for revolutionary societies, used to the freer atmosphere of Paris, to function. Despite these hardships, Engels decided to move to Brussels so that he and Marx could continue their political collaboration as well as their friendship.

Jenny Marx found life in Belgium pleasant, as she flourished within the small colony of German exiles. In April, to ease Jenny's second pregnancy, her mother sent her a servant, Helene Delmuth, or "Lenchen" as the Marx family called her. She would remain with the family for forty years, often working without pay, when there was no money for her wages. She ran the Marx household and was one of the few people around Marx who was not terrified by his temper. She often gave him sound, practical advice on political matters for she had the gift of organization that he lacked. She was a cheerful woman with a good sense of humor.

During the spring of 1845, Karl Marx resumed his writing, preparing his *Theses on Feuerbach.* Ludwig Feuerbach (1804–1872) was a philosopher who had argued that people made history, not God. While Marx agreed with this position, he criticized Feuerbach for failing to recognize that what people did was determined by their social class. Feuerbach had maintained that people's behavior could be explained in terms of generalized qualities, common to the human species. Marx insisted that if society could be changed, human relationships would be changed. For him, only revolution could bring those changes.

During the summer, Jenny traveled to Trier to be with her mother while Marx and Engels took a brief trip to England, where Engels conducted business at his father's textile mills in Manchester. In that famous industrial city, the two men spent time at the Chetham Library, reading the works of well-known English economists. On their way home, when they visited London, Marx and Engels met a group of German exiles who had formed a revolutionary society. It was modeled on the secret League of the Just, part of a French revolutionary tradition. In England, radical societies flourished without undue surveillance or suspicion. The more open English branch of the League of the Just took the name German Workers' Education Society. It sponsored political lectures and cultural events, a combination appealing to German refugees, most of whom were skilled artisans, not manual laborers. The League did not have a clear-cut political program. It was more a fraternal association of workers than a political group. Its members, however, saw themselves as dedicated revolutionaries. Yet, in their political schemes, they were visionaries or dreamers, not practical politicians or secret conspirators. They were to play a major part in Marx's life.

When Marx returned to Brussels in September 1845, Jenny gave birth to a second daughter, Laura, and he began work with Engels on *The German Ideology*. In this book they attacked revolutionary thinkers of the time who in Marx's opinion did not go far enough. The two friends were involved in this project well into the year 1846. Yet they could not find a publisher for such a long, argumentative book. The manuscript was not published in its entirety until 1962.

From the time he arrived in Brussels, Marx was an object of interest to Prussian police spies who reported to Berlin on his activities. The Prussian government also put pressure on the Belgian government to expel him as a radical revolutionary. Marx feared that he would be forced to leave Brussels, much as he had been forced to leave Paris. He grew so resentful of this harassment that he formally renounced his Prussian citizenship. In doing so, he became a stateless person, with no official status under international law, a permanent wandering alien. Marx had not anticipated the consequences of his action and eventually came to regret it.

In 1846, inspired by the German Workers' Education Society in London, Marx and Engels tried to set up a Communist Correspondence Committee to unify socialist ideas among German, French, and English radicals. Engels traveled to Paris to serve as the Committee's propagandist since Paris was in the mainstream of radical movements whereas Brussels was not. However, he soon grew disenchanted and returned to Brussels to enjoy the intellectual stimulation and companionship of his friend Karl Marx. Marx and Engels soon took over the newspaper *Deutsche-Brusseler Zeitung (German-Belgian Times)* and turned it into a platform for their views.

The Communist Correspondence Committee disbanded, to be replaced by the Communist League, also known as the German Workers Association. During this period communist organizations were constantly formed, disbanded, and reorganized under a series of different names. In part, the frequent reshufflings of members and names were a way of evading government authorities. Also, doctrinal disagreements and personality conflicts within the organizations caused members to leave and form their own splinter groups. Under Marx and Engels' sponsorship, the Communist League in Brussels met twice weekly to spread communist ideas and to sponsor events such as dances and songfests.

Unfortunately, Marx's inability to distinguish social from political relationships turned League meetings into political sparring matches. He developed intense relationships and then turned on his associates when they disagreed with him, usually because he advocated new directions and a more complete overhaul of society than they envisioned. The Russian Pavel Annenkov left a description of Marx's behavior during this time. "His movements were clumsy but bold and self-assured; his manners defied all usual social conventions. . . . He spoke in nothing but imperatives, the words tolerating no opposition, penetrating everything he said with a harsh tone that jarred me painfully." It was thus that Marx first cultivated and then turned on Wilhelm Weitling, a German theorist and a follower of his. Hermann Kriege, a journalist, was next. Marx also lost the friendship of Moses Hess, a longtime friend. In this way, Marx, supported by Engels, came to dominate the Brussels communist circle, a pattern to be repeated over and over again during his lifetime.

As part of his purification process, the purge of all who disagreed with him, Marx parted company with Proudhon, whom he had earlier invited to become a member of the Communist Correspondence Committee. His attack on Proudhon took the form of a book entitled *The Poverty of Philosophy*, cleverly reversing the title of Proudhon's major work, *The Philosophy of Poverty*. It took him the better part of 1846 and part of 1847 to complete. In it Marx rebuked Proudhon for his lack of a sense of history and for his naive solutions to human ills. He felt that Proudhon failed to understand economics and was all too willing to compromise with the existing institutions and practices of society; that is, Proudhon was a reformer, not a true revolutionary.

At the insistence of Engels, in November 1847, Marx set out to attend the second congress of the London Communist League, formerly known as the League of the Just. Marx traveled to meet Engels, who had gone on ahead. At the meeting in London, Marx gave a speech urging the English workers to lead the workers of the world in revolution. His speech was described as direct and to the point. By the beginning of December, Marx and Engels were able to convince the delegates to the congress to adopt their views of revolution, rather than reform, and to unite to work for a society run by and for workers without classes or private property. As the meetings drew to a close, the congress asked Marx to prepare a theoretical and practical platform for the organization.

Marx set to work on the project shortly after he returned from London in mid-December 1847. Just days after he arrived home, Jenny gave birth to their first son, Edgar. When she recovered from the delivery, she performed secretarial tasks for her busy husband. Marx also enlisted Engels' help with the writing. Thus the two men are now given credit for the work. Despite pleas and threats from the Central Committee of the congress, Marx and Engels took a long time preparing what was to become their masterpiece, the *Communist Manifesto*. They did not finish it until the end of January 1848.

The *Communist Manifesto* is remembered to this day, even when many of Marx and Engels' other writings are forgotten or ignored. In this work, they set forth the reasons why workers were mistreated and underpaid. They offered economic, social, and historical arguments to support the idea that workers had to rebel rather than reform society in order to gain power. Marx and Engels urged workers of all nations to join together in a revolution to make people truly equal. They wanted a world where all could enjoy the fruits of their own labors according to their needs and not according to who they were or who their fathers were.

The *Manifesto* contained theoretical justifications for the authors' claims, but at the same time, it provided a practical platform of action, such as doing away with private property and inheritance, which made some people in society appear to be superior to others. This is one of the most readable of Marx and Engels' works, probably because they addressed themselves to workers, rather than theorists and philosophers. Right after the publication of the *Manifesto*, a revolutionary storm swept Europe. While it is tempting to link the publication of this revolutionary tract with the events that immediately followed, there was in fact no connection.

This had been a most productive period in Marx's life. What had started in 1843 as a sojourn in France to write articles, to meet new people, and to exchange ideas had become an intellectual pilgrimage. Marx had begun to formulate his own theories of the role workers played in the existing society, and of the importance of revolution as a means of changing the political, social, and economic system. He had also begun to develop his own visions of a brave new society to follow in the wake of the old. As his circle of acquaintances broadened, Marx drifted farther away from the Young Hegelians. He made a lifelong friend and collaborator of Friedrich Engels, with whom he could share his dreams and take preliminary steps to bring them about. However, the price he paid for his opposition to the established order was high. He was condemned, because of his revolutionary thoughts and words as well as his political associations and affiliations, to a life of exile and poverty.

CHAPTER THREE
MARX IN REVOLT

In 1848, a series of revolutions swept Europe. They occurred spontaneously, without international plotting or planning. They were a genuine outburst of feelings that had been building up since the 1830s. Unmet demands for constitutional government, for the right to vote, for civil liberties, increased the frustration of those prevented from participating in the political life of their countries. In many parts of Europe, people became more aware of their common ancestry and pressed claims to govern themselves in their own states drawn on ethnic or national lines. They no longer wished to be ruled from above by those who did not share their cultural heritage, language, or religious beliefs. In contrast, others fought so that their shattered, fragmented little states would be unified into one strong central state.

It was a time of turmoil. The revolutions first erupted in France in February of 1848 with demands for democratic and constitutional government. Under the government of King Louis-Philippe, only one man in thirty could vote. When demands for electoral reform were not met, rioting broke out and Louis-Philippe abdicated his throne. A Provisional Government was set up to take charge and to organize the Second French Republic. The Provisional Government established National Workshops, organizations designed to provide public works projects, such as digging roads, for unemployed workers. In April a Constituent Assembly was elected to replace the Provisional Government.

By June, Paris experienced class warfare. The workers, organized in National Workshops, and the middle class, represented in the Constituent Assembly, fought each other for power. The workers were interested in social reforms, such as improved working conditions, while the middle classes wanted only political reforms, such as the extension of the suffrage. The Constituent Assembly was temporarily driven out by the angry workers, but a National Guard, a civilian militia, restored them to power. The Assembly declared martial law and turned their power to govern over to General Cavaignac and the regular army. Paris became the scene of bloody battles as the army fought the workers to restore order.

At the end of 1848, Louis-Napoleon Bonaparte (1808-1873) was voted into office with the support of the peasants and lower middle class, who had been terrified by the workers' demands and the resulting bloodshed. They were more interested in order than in reform and were willing to place a strong man in power to accomplish their goal. The Second Republic was on the verge of becoming the Second Empire.

By March 1848 the Austrian empire of the Hapsburgs felt the effects of nationalist revolutionary fervor. In Italy, Hungary, and Bohemia (today's Czechoslovakia), the people, resentful of Austrian rule, tried to establish separate states of their own. However, by December, the imperial army, supported by the aristocracy and the Catholic clergy, was able to reassert control. Instead of a compromise federation which would have been equally intolerable to the nationalist movements as well as to the Hapsburgs, Austria attempted to impose a centralized unitary system of rule over its subject peoples.

By March of 1848, a number of German governments collapsed as revolution swept many reigning princes and dukes from power. Arrangements were made for the election of an all-German assembly, the Frankfurt Assembly, to meet in the hope of creating a national government to fill the void. From May 1848 to May 1949, the assembly attempted to unify Germany. However, it was faced with resistance from the surviving petty German rulers. Also, it was unclear how the new Germany's borders were to be drawn. The final stumbling block was Prussia, the most powerful German state. The assembly offered the crown of a unified Germany-to-be to the king of Prussia, Frederick William IV, but he rejected it. He did not want his country to be absorbed into a larger Germany except on his own terms. He would not risk war with those German states the assembly did not include or with Hapsburg Austria, which sought to lead and control the states of Germany. In effect the assembly was doomed to failure because it could not gain the support of the larger German states.

The Frankfurt Assembly came to an end when the lower classes began to riot. They were demanding broader, more sweeping reforms than the middle-class assembly was prepared to accept. Lacking power, the Assembly had to depend on the Prussian army to restore order and keep the peace. Most members of the Assembly returned home, but a few diehards lingered on.

Meanwhile in Berlin, the capital city of Prussia, rioting broke out at the same time that other German states were toppling and plans were being made to summon the ill-fated Frankfurt Assembly. The Prussian king promised a constitution and allowed an elected legislature, the National Assembly, to be called into being. However, he ordered that assembly dissolved in December 1848. In 1850, the king finally issued his own constitution. Landowners and, later, industrialists were to benefit most from this political system, in which the right to vote was limited to a narrow circle. With the appointment of Count Otto von Bismarck (1815–1898) as chief minister of Prussia in 1862, Prussia was to become the core of a unified, centralized German empire. The dreams of the Frankfurt Assembly passed into history.

When the people of Paris took to the streets in February 1848, Marx welcomed the news. He expected the revolution to travel to Belgium, where he was still living. In preparation for this event, he lectured secret groups of workers on how to rebel. Using money his mother sent him from his father's legacy, he began to arm Belgian workers. This is another example of Marx's well-known indifference to money matters. He could have used the funds to give his family a much needed nest egg, but as usual, he gave revolutionary activities top priority.

Naturally, during these troubled times, the Belgian police had kept foreigners under even closer surveillance than usual. Spies within the German exile community kept them informed of the new funds at Marx's disposal and of Marx's secret activities. The police were particularly interested in Marx because he had given his word to stay out of Belgian politics. They became suspicious of Marx's sudden wealth, probably believing that the funds were smuggled in from French revolutionaries.

The Belgians proceeded to round up the radicals and troublemakers in order to avert a possible uprising. On March 3, Marx was ordered to leave Belgium within twenty-four hours. That night the police arrested him, claiming that he lacked proper papers. Jenny rushed to get him a lawyer, but she, too, was placed under arrest when she returned home. When the matter finally got sorted out, the twenty-four-hour time limit had run out. Leaving their possessions with a friend, including some silver Jenny had been given by her family, the Marx family left Belgium. They were escorted by the Belgian police until they reached the border of France. Fortunately, on March 3, Karl Marx had received an invitation from the Provisional Government of France to visit the country from which he had earlier been expelled. Otherwise, he would have had nowhere to go. Marx was a stateless person. When his permit to stay in Belgium was abruptly canceled, he lacked proper credentials of citizenship.

The Marx family returned to Paris just as National Workshops were being set up to provide employment for the jobless, and the revolution seemed to be succeeding. The family visited old acquaintances, such as the Herweghs and Heinrich Heine, whom they found in failing health. With the uprising in Berlin and the Prussian king's promise of a constitution, German exiles in Paris grew excited. Marx's old friend the poet Georg Herwegh had decided to put together a voluntary troop of German refugees to return to their homeland. Marx disapproved of this scheme because the troop was to fight for liberal reforms, not for the overthrow of the German social and economic system. Moreover, he felt that it would fail in its mission because the refugees were poorly trained and ill-equipped to do battle against the Prussian army. Events proved him right.

Marx sent for Engels, who had remained in Brussels. While in Paris, they attempted to organize a Communist League in Germany. They sought to get the German peasants, workers, and small shopkeepers to cooperate with them to bring about changes. The changes Marx and Engels had in mind were somewhat more radical than the liberal reforms being proposed but far more moderate than the aims stated in the *Communist Manifesto*. For example, no mention was made of abolishing private property, eliminating the right of inheritance, or requiring compulsory labor for all. Unlike Georg Herwegh and his associates, Marx chose to use the tool of propaganda, not weapons, to rouse the underprivileged sectors of society.

With Engels' help, he prepared a leaflet, "Demands of the Communist Party in Germany," for the Communist League. These demands included a united Germany, nationalization of transportation, public education, universal military service, restrictions on the right of inheritance, the issuance of valid paper currency, and separation of church and state. Liberal members of the Frankfurt Assembly, which was shortly to convene, would not find these proposals dangerously radical.

Marx had determined that the time was not yet ripe for a true socialist revolution. Germany's workers were still a small minority of the population. There was much to be accomplished in making the Prussian government responsive to the citizens before taking up the workers' special needs. Moreover, reforming the Prussian government would benefit everyone.

Marx believed that Paris, not Berlin, was where true revolutionary progress was to be made. After all, the workers of Paris had at least temporarily achieved National Workshops, recognized by the Provisional Government—even though the function of those workshops was to be disputed. Ardent socialists, such as Louis Blanc (1811–1882), whose idea they were, saw them as the possible foundation of a socialist society. Blanc had intended the workshops to be state-supported manufacturing establishments to be run and operated by the workers themselves. The liberals in the Provisional Government treated them as unemployment centers, and their view prevailed. It wasn't long before the Provisional Government, in an effort to extend its control, had the National Guard attempt to disband these centers.

Both Marx and Herwegh were seeking to gain the support of exiled German workers in Paris. Apparently these workers decided that helping Marx to establish a Communist League in Germany was not as attractive as joining Herwegh's troop, a more active and direct way to wage revolution. Since so many refugees were returning to Germany to fight for change, Marx chose to return to his native land to pursue his plan for a Communist League. With Engels, Marx moved to Cologne, where he had lived in 1842. Upon his arrival, Marx applied for citizenship and the right to live in the city. He was allowed to remain, but his application for citizenship was denied. His family, meanwhile, moved to Trier to be with Jenny's mother. They joined him three months later, but Marx had little time for family life.

At the time Marx and Engels arrived in Cologne, this industrial city was the third largest in Prussia, with a history of opposition to Prussian rule and to monarchical government in general. In Cologne, about a fourth of the working force was unemployed. From their base in the city, Marx and Engels sent out emissaries to determine the strength of the Communist League in other German cities. They learned that it was virtually nonexistent.

After the failure of their Communist League, Marx and Engels were invited to become members of a local communist organization, the Cologne Workers' Association. It had been founded and led by Andreas Gottschalk, a physician. Marx rejected the offer, for he could not accept Gottschalk's views of the events taking place in Germany. Gottschalk had objected to the elections then being held for the Frankfurt Assembly. He was pinning his hopes on a workers' social revolution. Marx still maintained that the time was not yet ripe for such an undertaking. He parted company with Gottschalk and formed the Cologne Democratic Association in an attempt to enlist the support of Germans from many walks of life. He also went ahead with plans he and Engels had formulated in Paris to start a newspaper in Cologne. Its readership was to be Marx's true party.

Despite overwhelming financial difficulties, Marx and Engels launched the *Neue Rheinische Zeitung (New*

Rhine Times) and printed the first edition by June 1, 1848. In Engels' words, "The organization of the editorial staff was a simple dictatorship by Marx." This statement is most illuminating. It reveals, once again, Marx's need to dominate, to be in control, and perhaps explains why he refused to support Herwegh's troop or join Gottschalk's workers. He would play second fiddle to no one, nor would he compromise his revolutionary principles by taking premature steps to carry them out. On the other hand, he would not completely identify himself with liberal reformers' plans either.

By charting an independent course and refusing to compromise, he managed to antagonize Carl Schurz (1829–1906), the young German liberal reformer who eventually became a United States senator. Marx and Schurz met during the summer of 1848 at a conference of democratic associations held in Cologne. Later Schurz wrote of him, "I have never seen a man whose bearing was so provoking and intolerable. . . . Everyone who contradicted him he treated with abject contempt."

Marx intended to use his newspaper to help bring into existence a democratic Germany. He wanted to participate in the politics of the day to make news, not merely report it. So he wrote incendiary articles prodding Germans to end absolutism, feudalism, and all the other trappings of the Prussian government. Seeking to widen support for his views, he said not a word about the workers or socialism.

In his articles, Marx took the police to task for the manner in which they arrested Friedrich Anneke, a communist, implying that at least one of the officers was drunk. He satirized Prussian aristocrats by publishing a piece written by George Weerth describing the supposed exploits of a Prince Schnapphahnski. He reported on the prospect of a new censorship law, predicting that if it went into effect the Prussian government would be able to commit any outrage with impunity. His earlier defenses of a free press had been far more philosophical. He even criticized the Frankfurt Assembly, which he called a "talking shop." Marx now saw his role as that of a gadfly, pointing out injustices and moral outrages wherever they occurred.

Marx used his French papers to obtain a travel permit to visit Berlin, Vienna, Prague, and Dresden, where he talked to leaders of the liberal reform movement rather than to workers' organizations. He was hoping to make these leaders more receptive to moral pressure from the masses of the German people and used his newspaper to foster that pressure. Marx seemed to feel that by cooperating with reformers the workers might gain more than by demonstrating or rioting, which would frighten them and drive them into the embrace of the repressive forces of the old order.

As the forces of restoration and repression appeared to be gaining strength, so Marx's newspaper articles took on a more radical tone. In September, he urged workers to attend a large public meeting to protest military brutality. Another demonstration by workers and socialists on the outskirts of Cologne four days later led the authorities to declare martial law and to issue arrest warrants for Engels and six others, but not for Karl Marx. Although he had appeared at the demonstrations, and had even been elected to a newly created Public Safety Committee the workers' leaders had formed, he had not been linked to radical workers' movements.

Engels, fearful of arrest and desperately short of funds, went to Barmen, where he met with his parents. His father complained to him that he did not want to have a revolutionary for a son. His mother warned him that the family would not continue to give him financial support if he persisted in his revolutionary activities. Heeding his parents' wishes, Engels escaped from Germany to wander through France. He did not return to Cologne until January.

After the arrest warrants were issued, Marx addressed an association of workers, arguing against violence and revolutionary fervor. The time was still not ripe for revolution as Marx saw it. Because Cologne was under martial law, his newspaper was temporarily shut down, but it resumed publication in October.

In November, the Prussian army marched on the National Assembly. Moving to a hotel, members of the Assembly voted a resolution urging Prussians not to pay their taxes. Marx seized the occasion to publicize their appeal to all the people of Germany. Needless to say, by publicizing this appeal, Marx did not gain favor with the Prussian government. In December, he managed to antagonize Prussian officials even further when he criticized the king for dissolving the National Assembly.

It is not surprising that Marx was soon ordered to appear in court to face charges. First, he was accused of having insulted members of the police and the aristocratic class in articles he had written. Secondly, he was charged with inciting people to rebel by writing about the antitax campaign. Fortunately for Marx, Cologne's law was based on the Napoleonic Code. Unlike Prussian law, it required that Marx be tried by a jury. The Napoleonic Code, enacted in France in 1804, unified previously diverse and contradictory laws into one clear set of rules. It listed the rights of individuals, protected private property, and established laws governing contracts. The code was adopted by many European countries.

Marx's trial was set for February 1849. He was escorted to the courthouse by a crowd of sympathizers, to whom he made his only two public speeches in Cologne. In the courtroom he defended himself against the first charge by claiming that the laws concerning insults only referred to spoken words, not printed ones. In response to the second charge, he claimed that he was not a revolutionary and had simply represented the common cause. The jury acquitted him!

By this time, Marx's newspaper was virtually bankrupt, its articles having offended potential backers from every part of the political spectrum. What's more, he was no longer a Prussian citizen. Although Marx had applied for citizenship during his stay in Cologne, the Prussian authorities had rejected his request. His only proof of identity was a French passport issued in March 1848. With his legal status in constant jeopardy from the increasingly provocative and controversial articles he wrote, Karl Marx set out in April to visit Hamburg, Bremen, and Berlin to see if he could raise funds among liberal reformers so that he could continue to publish his newspaper. He met with little success.

While he was traveling, an official in Cologne prepared papers ordering Marx's expulsion from Prussia. They were to be served on him in mid-May. All that was needed was an excuse. On May 10, Marx printed an article that not only condemned the reigning king of Prussia but the whole dynasty. Since the king had dissolved the Assembly, and the army had restored order in Baden and the Ruhr, where there had been revolts, officials felt that it was time to remove a thorn from their sides. The article gave them that excuse. The order of expulsion was delivered to Karl Marx on May 16. Jenny Marx busily disposed of the family's household effects while her husband sold his printing presses, settled accounts with printers, and provided travel money to his fellow editors, who were also ordered to leave Germany. The Marx family and Friedrich Engels traveled to Frankfurt to stay temporarily with friends. Here Jenny pawned the family silver once again and from the proceeds, she financed a trip to Trier for herself, Lenchen, and the children.

During their travels through Germany to make arrangements for Marx's return to France, both Marx and Engels were briefly arrested by Hessian troops, who suspected them of participating in a local revolt. Upon their release, Marx set out for France under an assumed name, M. Ramboz, while Engels enlisted with the military forces of the provisional government of Baden, which was trying to resist the onslaught of Prussian troops. In July, when the king's forces inevitably triumphed, Engels escaped to Switzerland. From there he made his way to England.

The days of the Second French Republic had passed, and the autocratic Louis-Napoleon was tightening his control over the country. In 1851–1852 Marx would write *The Eighteenth Brumaire of Louis Bonaparte* in which he brilliantly analyzed the social coalition made up of peasants and small shopkeepers, groups that had felt threatened by the power of the middle and upper classes in the Second Republic and had been terrified by the workers. This social coalition had brought Louis-Napoleon to power.

With his reputation as a radical, Marx could no longer expect to be greeted as a welcome visitor. When he arrived in France, the French police were already on his trail. To make matters worse, a cholera epidemic had broken out in Paris, where Marx hid out as M. Ramboz. He was burdened by poverty and troubled by the news that Jenny was expecting yet another child. In the beginning of July, she had joined him with Lenchen and the children. The family was penniless and sick. There was little left to be taken to the pawnshop and exchanged for the funds necessary to buy food or pay the rent. It may have almost seemed a relief when on July 19th the French police presented Marx with an order requiring him to leave Paris. He was to be banished to the French department of Morihan, in Brittany, a prospect that failed to please him. To him, Brittany was the middle of nowhere, a backwater setting away from the mainstream of politics. Of course, that was what the French probably had in mind.

Marx was given a few days grace to decide whether he would comply with the order or leave France altogether.

His choices were narrow. He could not return to Germany, and the Swiss denied him a passport. By default Marx opted to join Engels in London. At the age of thirty-one, he left France for good. On August 26 he set out for England, which was to be his home for the rest of his life. He was a refugee without prospects, without money, without a career.

The door slammed shut on an important part of Marx's life. Never again would he witness a revolution in the making, never again would he publish a newspaper, never again would he take an active role in political life. The revolutions of 1848 had raised his hopes for the future, but even at the height of the furor Marx had chosen a relatively moderate path. He had decided to cooperate with the reforming elements of society rather than with the radical revolutionaries. He had abandoned the workers for the middle classes in the hope that through the successes of the latter, the former might benefit. He sensed that it would be premature for workers to attempt to seize control of the social and political system, no matter how promising and tempting at times that prospect appeared. His studies had convinced him that the forces of absolutism and repression had to be routed and replaced by democratic, constitutional regimes before the workers' hopes could be realized. So he devoted his energies and his talents to bringing this less drastic change about, but it would be the last time that he cooperated with a middle-class movement. He became disillusioned with their endless debates and their lack of accomplishments. By 1849 the forces of the old order had triumphed, but Marx knew that their victories would not last forever. He expected revolutions to recur in his lifetime. Sustained by this belief, he left for England to devote his life to the development of his theories of revolution and social change.

CHAPTER FOUR
MARX
IN EXILE

Perhaps because England had a representative government which gradually undertook needed reforms, the nation was spared the bloodshed and disruption that accompanied the revolutions of 1848 in continental Europe. From 1837 to 1901, Queen Victoria sat on the throne of England, a symbol of continuity amid change. As early as 1832, a reform act had increased the number of voters in the British electorate by almost 50 percent so that those with small amounts of property could participate in elections. A further expansion of the electorate came in 1867, when the rest of the middle class and many workers finally got the right to vote. More importantly, the 1832 reform act had redistributed seats in Parliament so that the growing industrial cities of England had a more just share of parliamentary representation. Prior to 1832 landed interests and agricultural centers had dominated Parliament.

It was the industrial revolution that had created the greatest amount of dislocation and upheaval in English society as well as the greatest need for reforms. Coal powered the machinery of industry, which produced the textiles that brought factory owners much wealth. In 1842 government investigating committees revealed that children as young as three years of age were working in the coal mines. Both women and children were chained to carts used to drag the mined coal through tunnels too narrow for adult males to use. It is no wonder that the government at long last prohibited underground employment of women, and girls and boys under ten years of age.

Conditions in textile factories were no better than those in the mines. An act of 1833 had required that no children under age thirteen work more than forty-eight hours a week. No person under eighteen was to work more than sixty-nine hours a week. An hour and a half each day was to be set aside for meals, and children were to attend school for at least two hours a day. Yet in 1841, a government committee reported that children at work making lace were not permitted to go home for meals or to attend school. Instead they were kept at their looms day after day. It wasn't until 1847 that the Ten Hour Act was passed, limiting the hours women and young people could work in factories. By common practice, men began to work ten hours as well, even though their hours were not regulated by legislation.

Reform extended to include the necessities of life. Workers had been angered by the high cost of food that resulted from a tax on imported grain, known as the Corn Laws. These were finally repealed in 1846 after a decade of protest. Little, however, was done about the crowded slums where workers lived, where sanitation was poor, and the spread of disease often reached epidemic proportions.

It was into this world of change that Karl Marx arrived in the late summer of 1849. Both he and Engels had thought that their stay in England would be short, that the tide of revolution that had swept Europe would surge forth once again. With this in mind, Marx rejoined the Communist League in London. In 1850 he presented the League with "An Address," intended to console the defeated participants in the 1848 struggles. He urged them to look to the future, for surely new revolutions would soon break out. He recommended that in future revolutions they no longer cooperate with liberal reformers but rather set up their own governments side by side with the liberals. That way they would not be neglected or shunted aside. He had not forgotten his recent experiences with liberal reformers in Cologne.

As hope for new revolutionary outbreaks faded, the more militant communists, such as August von Willich, wanted to spark their own revolutions. They ridiculed Marx as a thinker rather than a doer. Marx gradually withdrew from their meetings as he had during the turmoil of 1848. By 1851 he seemed to have abandoned the League. In November 1852, it was dissolved.

In politics, Marx had experienced disappointment and isolation, but there were some compensations to life in London. Unlike Brussels, Paris, or Cologne, there was no censorship, no police surveillance. Citizens and refugees alike enjoyed political freedom. London was a cosmopolitan city where strangers could feel at home. There was a large refugee community and plenty of places for refugees to meet. There were the cultural advantages of a capital city, including free concerts, museums, parks, and libraries. Even though the Marx family could enjoy the advantages London had to offer, they were also to endure years of tragedy and despair.

By September 17, 1849, Jenny and the Marx children arrived in London. They spent their first winter crowded into a single, dilapidated room. On November 5, Guy Fawkes Day, Jenny gave birth to a boy, Edmund Heinrich, who was soon nicknamed Guido in honor of the English holiday. The Marx family enjoyed giving nicknames to each other and to family friends. For example,

Karl Marx was often called "the Moor" because of his dark coloring. His daughter Laura was often called "Hottentot," his son, Edgar, "Musch." The family often referred to Engels as "the General," in honor of his military action in Baden, while another friend, Wilhelm Liebknecht, was called "Library," because he was rarely seen without books in his arms.

In his accounts of Karl Marx during the 1850s, Liebknecht offered a portrait of a happy, close family despite its disappointments and hardships. He expressed a sense of puzzlement that Marx could use such violent and forceful language when discussing politics, and yet with his family, his tone was usually gentle and kind. He could be a domineering father, however, and he was known to have terrible rages. The rages were probably the result of his political setbacks and his inability to support his family. Lenchen could quickly calm him down, and a look from Jenny would freeze him on the spot.

Jenny could be very commanding in her own right when it came to matters of proper behavior, decorum, and manners. It is claimed that she never quite approved of Marx's friendship with Friedrich Engels. She objected to Engels' carefree womanizing, to his long-term relationship with Mary Burns. To escape from her behavioral code, Marx would occasionally join friends and wander from pub to pub, drinking a full glass of beer in each establishment.

On Sundays, Liebknecht wrote, the family would take off for one of the London parks with picnic hamper in tow. Refugee friends frequently joined them on these outings. There would be songs, laughter, and even donkey rides, when funds permitted, but Marx could barely carry a tune and astride a donkey he was an object of some ridicule.

While the Marx family enjoyed good times together, their early years in London were desperate and tragic. The baby, Guido, was sickly. To add to their woes, in

April 1850, while Jenny was feeding him, the landlady burst in and demanded the rent money. The family did not have it so they desperately tried to sell their few possessions. Still lacking the needed funds, they had to suffer the indignity of eviction, the first of many. There were to be quite a few changes of address.

Poverty continued to take its toll in terms of illness, death, and despair. Jenny, pregnant once again, traveled to Holland to appeal in person to her husband's uncle Lion Philips for funds, but the prosperous businessman was unwilling to support his radical, revolutionary nephew. Money could have purchased decent housing, nutritious food, and medical help. Unfortunately, enough money to live decently, if modestly, was not to be had. By November 1850 Guido was dead, a victim of pneumonia brought on by the family's extreme poverty. In March 1851, Jenny gave birth to a daughter, Francesca. At that time, Lenchen was also pregnant. She had a son she named Freddy. Although Marx was actually the father, Engels claimed Freddy as his own to spare Jenny further grief. By now, Jenny was often hysterical and depressed, and tragedy continued to strike the Marx family. During Easter 1852, Francesca died of severe bronchitis. The undertakers would not extend credit so Jenny dashed about trying to borrow money for the tiny coffin.

A Prussian spy who visited the two-room Marx household in 1852 described it by saying, "In the whole apartment there is not one clean and solid piece of furniture. Everything is broken, tattered, and torn, with a half inch of dust over everything and great disorder everywhere. . . . A seller of secondhand goods would be ashamed to give away such a remarkable collection of odds and ends."

In March 1855, Marx's only surviving son, Edgar, was diagnosed as having tuberculosis. He died in April of that year. Jenny, having just given birth to another daughter, Eleanor, was overwhelmed with grief; Marx's hair turned white. When Marx wrote about poverty and hopelessness in his philosophical tracts, he wasn't presenting an abstract, impersonal account. He had experienced the effects of poverty firsthand and knew how devastating it could be.

Between 1852 and 1862, the little money Marx was able to earn came from his post as a foreign correspondent for *The New York Tribune*. The *Tribune* was published by Horace Greeley. Its managing editor was Charles Dana, who had met Marx in 1848 when Marx ran the *Neue Rheinische Zeitung* in Cologne and Dana was reporting on the European revolutions. In August 1851, Dana wrote to Marx inviting him to write for the *Tribune*. His articles would appeal to the German immigrants who were flocking to the United States. Marx would be able to present his views without having to worry about government censorship. This seemed like an ideal arrangement except that Marx found it difficult at first to write in English. He had to depend on Engels to translate and sometimes even to substitute for him. In all, Engels wrote about a quarter of the articles attributed to Marx. However, over time, Marx learned to express himself well in this foreign tongue.

Marx's stories were more impressionistic than investigative, since he relied on English newspapers and official reports found in the British Museum. There was little observation or direct reporting in Marx's articles. He chose political rather than economic topics and seemed to prefer to write about foreign rather than domestic affairs. When the United States approached the eve of the Civil War, interest in foreign affairs waned. Dana parted company with Greeley, and Marx found himself writing less and less. Consequently his earnings tapered off.

The *Tribune* provided Marx with the only regular income he earned while he lived in England. Until 1864, when Engels became a partner in his father's Manchester textile mill, he could do little to assist Marx, as his own earnings were meager. Once he became financially secure, he was most generous and helpful to the Marx family. From 1869 on, he contributed 350 pounds sterling a year to Marx and his family. Even in the midst of their terrible poverty, Marx seemed unwilling or unable to get a steady job. The family did receive a small legacy when Jenny's mother died in 1856, but all it did was enable them to move to new quarters.

In 1861, Marx traveled to Holland, where he was finally able to persuade his uncle to help him repay some of his most pressing debts. From there he traveled to Berlin, where he was the guest of socialist journalist Ferdinand Lassalle (1825–1864), to negotiate about the editorship of a newspaper in Berlin. Marx was able to travel to Berlin because the Prussian king, Wilhelm I (1797–1888), had given an amnesty to political exiles, but when he tried to reclaim his Prussian citizenship, the officials would give him only a passport good for one year. Perhaps for this reason, as well as the fact that his wife had opposed the prospect of returning to Germany, Marx left Berlin. After a brief visit to his mother in Trier, he returned to England.

In 1864 Marx received a fairly large sum bequeathed to him by his friend Wilhelm Wolff, and at the same time he was given the rest of his inheritance from his mother, who had recently died. Yet Marx and his family were impractical and knew little about managing funds. What they had, they spent, neither wisely nor well. With the bequests they received in 1864, they moved to a large house. Money quickly disappeared.

Jenny, Laura, and Eleanor were trained in all the accomplishments proper Victorian young ladies were expected to have, such as reading, singing, and dancing. The Marx household took on the air of genteel middle-class respectability. Marx took pride in his wife's aristocratic background and in the family possessions; but family valuables were often in pawnshops, since Marx did not provide the means to support the style of life he chose to lead. This portrait of the Marx family contrasts sharply with the attacks on middle-class family life to be found in Marx's writings.

During his first decade in England, Marx did not abandon all attempts at serious writing. He managed to complete his analysis of Louis Napoleon's France, *The Eighteenth Brumaire of Louis Bonaparte*, and in 1859, his first book on political economy, *A Contribution to the Critique of Political Economy*. He also wrote the little-known *Herr Vogt*, in 1860, refuting charges by a liberal Swiss professor that he was the head of a group of blackmailers.

In the decades that followed, Marx devoted most of his time to a detailed analysis of industrial society, its shortcomings, and its impact on people's lives. He was able to complete only the first volume of his complex and lengthy *Capital* before his death. It was published in 1867. Engels compiled the remaining two volumes from Marx's notes. Although Marx was a university-trained scholar, he confined his research to books and reports in the British Museum and failed to meet with the leading scholars of the day. His work contained the research and conclusions of a lifetime of learning and second-hand observations of factory life, supplied by Engels.

Marx's last venture into socialist politics took place in 1864 with the founding of the International Workingmen's Association, known as the First International. The organization was intended to coordinate the efforts of workers to bring about socialist systems in many countries. Marx had cut himself off from the socialist movement after the failure of the Communist League, so he was not involved in the decision to form the First International, but he did receive an invitation to attend its inaugural meeting in September. There he was appointed to a provisional committee, which became the General Council of the association, to work out a platform for the new movement. A majority of the council were prominent English trade union leaders, whom Marx regarded as reformers rather than revolutionaries. Although in ill health, Marx began to dominate the proceedings. His European supporters came to occupy key posts in the organization and gave him a base of support.

At the age of forty-six, Marx delivered the First International's "Inaugural Address," a moderate statement reflecting his deeper appreciation of British social and economic conditions. He praised English labor reform achievements as well as the level of English industrial output. He urged the workers to seek to gain political power to bring about further improvement in their lives. He also recommended that the membership develop a common foreign policy to protest and prevent wars and aggression and to defend workers' rights. Marx was advocating peaceful change, not violent revolution. Such moderation would appeal to the English trade unions, followers of Lassalle in Germany, of Proudhon in France, and others.

Although the International faced financial difficulties throughout its existence, its membership grew. Marx became its guiding spirit, developing ties with English trade unions and foreign visitors, and using the International as a platform for his views, much as he had used the *Neue Rheinische Zeitung*.

However, by 1868, the International developed internal dissension that eventually caused it to disband. At issue was tight discipline and a unified policy within the International or freedom of choice to meet local issues and local concerns. The interests and needs of the workers in the nations of Europe were far too diverse at this stage for a common policy to prevail. Marx began to clash with Russian exile Mikhail Bakunin, whom he had met earlier in Paris. Their disagreement was made worse by the fact that Marx identified Russia with the forces of repression. Bakunin and his anarchist supporters challenged Marx's leadership. Anarchists preached the use of terrorism and violence against authority, particularly government officials. They felt that governments were harmful and unnecessary. Marx had disavowed them.

While Marx was involved with the International, he did manage to write several pieces. His last major work was *The Civil War in France*, written in 1871. It concerned the uprising that took place after Prussia defeated France in 1870, when a provisional government in France struggled to bring the Third Republic into being. At that time, Parisian workers briefly undertook to establish an alternative government of their own. Marx analyzed the failure of this famous Paris Commune. With the 1870 Franco-Prussian War and the Paris Commune, the membership of the International was splintering into diverse groups.

At the Hague Congress of the International in 1872, Bakunin's supporters were expelled, but by then the struggle had virtually destroyed the organization. As a face-saving gesture, Engels proposed that its headquarters be moved to New York, removed from European politics, which brought the International effectively to an end.

Marx's health had begun to mirror the condition of the International. While never good, at this stage of his life his health only became worse. As a heavy smoker, he had suffered a number of respiratory ailments. He also endured his share of digestive complaints. At times, he suffered from boils, a painful skin eruption. He traveled from spa to spa throughout Europe, and even Algiers, seeking curative waters, but the treatments were not particularly successful. He also seemed to be suffering from mental depression and was unable to complete the work he undertook. He did prepare a *Critique of the Gotha*

Program in 1875, commenting on the platform of a newly formed German workers' party. He also wrote several other pieces, but he was aging rapidly and wrote less and less.

His final years were not happy ones. Two of his daughters had married, despite Marx's concern about their husbands' abilities to support them. Laura had married socialist Paul LaFargue in 1868; Jenny, Charles Longuet, a French newspaper editor, in 1872. It was, however, Eleanor, nicknamed "Tussy," who worried him. This beloved daughter, and sometime actress, seemed subject to bouts of mental depression. Some have suggested that her mental instability was the result of Karl Marx's persistent refusal to let her marry the man she loved, Hippolyte Prosper-Olivier Lissagaray, a Frenchman who had supported the Paris Commune. Perhaps Marx was reluctant to let Eleanor marry because he wanted her to serve as her parents' companion, as youngest daughters were often expected to do in those days.

Marx was even more concerned about the health of his wife, Jenny. She had been suffering great pain and in 1881 was finally diagnosed as having an incurable cancer of the liver. When she died in 1881, Marx was too weak to attend the funeral. Then his daughter Jenny, mother of his only grandchildren, died of cancer on January 11, 1883. On March 14, 1883, Karl Marx died, sitting in his easy chair, with faithful Lenchen in attendance. A bleeding lung tumor was the immediate cause of death. Laura and Eleanor were to take their own lives, Eleanor in 1898 and Laura in 1911.

Marx was buried in London in Highgate Cemetery next to his wife. Only a few people attended his funeral. Friedrich Engels delivered the eulogy. At the conclusion of his remarks, he said of his friend, "His name will endure through the ages, and so will his work!" Engels' prediction has come to pass. Marx's theory, in one form or another, has taken on a life of its own.

Part two discusses Marx's theory. It explains why Marx thought that it was historically inevitable that the working classes would come to power and create a new social and political order. This section examines Marx's views of history, the reasons why workers had a special mission to play as history advanced, the way they would gain power when the time was ripe, and finally the new society they would create. It explains his ideas and shows the strengths and weaknesses of his arguments.

PART TWO

MARXISM

THE THEORY

CHAPTER FIVE
HISTORY
AS A SCIENCE

While most people may agree to define history as the study of the past, they will probably disagree about how to interpret what happened in the past. There are indeed many ways to view the past and make sense of what happened then. Karl Marx had nothing in common with those who see history as a series of disconnected, random events. For them, each occurrence is unique and distinct with no link to what went before or will happen later on; they do not believe that history is something one can understand. Nor did Marx agree with people who view history as a cycle of neverending, recurring events, those who claim that "History repeats itself!" For them, there is nothing further to learn. What's more, he rejected the view that history is the unfolding of God's will or the forward march of time to some final day of judgment and doom. As was mentioned earlier, Marx was an atheist, so he felt that the future of humanity was in human, not divine, control.

Marx firmly believed that history was a proper subject for study. It could be understood and perhaps even mastered. He believed that history was moving toward a particular goal or destiny, so individual events were meaningful. They were meaningful as signposts pointing out the direction in which history was moving, or how far away the goal still was. Marx held a progressive view of history, that is, he believed that the course of history was going to improve things for humankind. However, Marx was concerned with life here on earth and not with some supernatural destiny, so his view of history is a secular one. Not only did Marx claim to have a progressive and secular view of history, he also insisted that his was a scientific approach to the study of the past.

Scientists study data in the hope of discovering rules which will enable them to predict what will happen next. They examine their material over and over again and expect that others will be able to repeat their efforts and draw the same conclusions. It is far more difficult to attempt to do this with human affairs. People's behavior will change in different circumstances, locations, and time periods, so the rules that are set up for one country, one society, or one generation can hardly be expected to apply to everyone, everywhere, for ever and ever.

Perhaps Marx misunderstood what scientists do, but then again, in the nineteenth century, scientific methods were not as exacting as they are today. In his day, many people were enthusiastic about the uses of science, even if their applications weren't as precise and accurate as their modern counterparts. So Marx should not be faulted for attempting to discover scientific laws that might apply to society. In setting out to formulate a scientific approach to the study of history, Marx intended to learn what the future goal of humanity was, what signposts to look for, and what steps would bring that goal nearer. To study history scientifically, Marx needed a method, a way of looking at all the big and small events that occur, arranging them in some kind of order, and interpreting his findings. The method he developed is called dialectical materialism.

Of all Marx's ideas, dialectical materialism is one of the most difficult to understand. Thus it makes sense to split this cumbersome concept in two, to take a look at what Marx meant by the word *dialectical* before trying to define *materialism*. Dialectic is related to a more familiar word, *dialogue*, or a conversation between people. Originally, when ancient Greeks used the term, *dialectic* was indeed a conversation between people who held contradictory views. The Greeks expected that as they discussed their different viewpoints, the truth would gradually emerge.

The philosopher Georg Hegel borrowed this ancient notion of getting at the truth and adapted it to historical change. For Hegel, as history unfolded, contradictory or opposing ideas would develop and gradually become reconciled. This process has often been described as the rise of a thesis, or main idea, such as the belief that the only people who were fit to rule nations were those whose fathers had ruled nations, the idea of the hereditary monarchy. Of course, while most people might accept this thesis for a time, eventually after a series of kings who were cruel or incapable, some doubters might come along, who would offer their own concept of leadership, an antithesis, or contrary opinion. The doubters might suggest a new idea, the idea that the only people fit to rule a nation were those who had the nation's best interests at heart and had an interest in the land and its people, the nobles, the notion of an aristocracy. Over time, a synthesis might arise wherein the notion of leadership was extended and changed to let the monarch and aristocrats share power to rule nations. This synthesis in turn would become the thesis for a later historical period when government by nobles and kings proved unsatisfactory. It would spark a new antithesis, the belief that the middle classes truly represented all the people and were the ones best able to exercise leadership. They were entitled to power.

According to Hegel, history was the field on which the battle of ideas and ideals was fought, interrupted only by temporary truces until the forces regrouped and new battles were waged. For Hegel, though, what was important was the ideas. Hegel felt that the clash and reconciliation of opposing ideas was the essence of history, not the tangible, real people, things, or events that these ideas represented. This is why Hegel is known as an idealist, or a person who believes that ideas are more real than objects or things. After all, ideas were perfect. They did not age, weaken, erode, or waste away.

In this sense, the idea of a table is more real than any table people use. The table people use can be made of wood, metal, or glass, but it is still a table. It can have three legs or four, but it is still a table. What's more, one of the legs may be wobbly and the top dented and marred with stains. In addition, it can be used for eating, talking, or even doing homework. What makes it a table and not something else, like a stool, or a desk, or a kitchen counter? For Hegel, what makes a table a table is the idea of a table and not people's imperfect attempts to construct or use one.

As a university student, Marx had been attracted to Hegel's theories. He was drawn to Hegel's theories of the dialectic, but gradually Marx rejected Hegel's idealism. For Marx, what counted was the actual table someone constructed and not the idea of what a table should be. In other words, Marx was a materialist, not an idealist. For him, material conditions, circumstances capable of being seen, touched, tasted, smelled, or heard, were the primary stuff of historical change, not ideas. Marx made use of Feuerbach's criticism of Hegel, which he had read as a university student. From his studies of history, Marx concluded that there could not be any truths or even ideas that applied throughout time. For him, everything depended upon historical circumstances, upon the material conditions of an age.

Take the notion of health, a hard concept to define under the best of circumstances. In an age when people were living under poor sanitary conditions and had less nutritious diets, being healthy could simply mean not suffering from contagious diseases, like the measles, the mumps, smallpox, and the plague. Technology today has eliminated the source of these illnesses and has even devised vaccines to prevent them from occurring. What's more, people today have more opportunities to eat balanced diets, to exercise, and to maintain personal cleanliness. Yet today, people can suffer the effects of exposure to radiation left by nuclear waste materials or to toxic chemicals, such as PCBs, or to dangerous substances, such as asbestos, problems people in Marx's day were spared. Today changed conditions require a new meaning for the concept of health.

Going back to the earlier example of competing ideas of leadership, Marx would not necessarily concern himself with the abstract beliefs behind the claims of monarchs, aristocrats, or middle classes to rule. He would look at the existing historical circumstances, who actually held power, and at the material conditions supporting that power. He would argue that when the conditions shifted, another group should and would come to power. The interesting question for Marx was the source of power and not the ideas that justified its use.

Marx held that the source of power lay in the material things of this world. He knew that some people had more and other people had less land, gold, food, clothes, furniture, and other necessities and luxuries of life. From Marx's point of view, those with more were certainly more powerful than those who had less. This led him to ask how the material things of this world are made and distributed. The answer lay in economics, the process by which goods and services are made and exchanged. Marx concluded that economics determined who had power and who did not.

Marx is known as an economic determinist because he believed that economics forms the basis of all human activities, providing the material conditions under which people live. For example, according to Marx's logic, in a traditional farming community, the start and end of children's school year is not based on some abstract theory of education, prescribing how many days of education a year students need to learn their lessons but rather on when the children are actually needed to help with the planting or harvest the crops.

On a broader scale, Marx actually argued that all the institutions of a society, from its government to life within its families, were the result of the way goods and services were made and exchanged. In a society where a few individuals held all the wealth, government was likely to be harsh and laws would be made to benefit and protect the interests of the wealthy few and not the numerous poor.

Where the poor were numerous, men, women, and even children would have to work long hours so that they had food to eat, clothes to wear, and a roof over their heads. In such families, there would be little time for leisure, learning, or loving. Economics would determine the circumstances and the quality of that family's life just as it determined the kinds of laws they had to obey. According to Marx, the shifting tides of economic forces and the hardships they caused people gave rise to the contradictions and reconciliations of the dialectic that caused history to change and progress, not some vague Hegelian ideas. This is what Marx meant by dialectical materialism.

As Marx studied the economic forces that determined the course of history, he singled out one factor as especially important because it answered the question of where power comes from. For Marx, that most important factor was ownership of the means of production. According to Marx's studies, the people who possessed the equipment and capacity to have things made were the most powerful people in any society. The owners of land, tools, machinery, or factories had the resources others needed to make things for the society so they had control over the people who actually made the goods or offered the services as well as control over people who bought the products or services. If a noble owned most of the land in a county, farmers would have to work for him or lease land from him. Thus ownership of the land gave the nobility power and control over the farmers. Similarly the owner of a factory with tools and machinery was more powerful than an individual skilled laborer who needed those tools and machinery to put his skills to use. To protect themselves, the nobles or the factory owners would use their power to control the government so that the laws promoted their interests, not those of the more numerous but less powerful farmers or laborers. In this way, those who owned the means of production, an economic group, or class within a society, sought to determine the direction that the history of a society would take.

However, Marx claimed that the interests of the powerful, the owners of the means of production, would be contrary to the interests of those who worked for them. He maintained that the haves and the have-nots had opposing views based on their differing economic interests. The conflict between those opposing interests were the very stuff of the dialectic that brought about historical change. That is why Marx insisted that all history was the history of class struggles, struggles between those who had and those who did not. As history progressed, the struggles resulted in greater freedom for those who were needy and oppressed. Gradually, the exploited would triumph over their exploiters.

He used his dialectical method to survey the clash between nobles, who owned the means of production, and serfs, who labored for them in feudal times, setting up a thesis and an antithesis. From the strife between nobles and serfs emerged a new synthesis, the rise of the middle class. In his own lifetime, Marx witnessed the emergence of a new class of have-nots, the workers who labored in the factories and plants owned by the middle class. He predicted that as history progressed, this group of have-nots would eventually triumph over those who held power over them. Since he could not foresee any group that these workers could oppress once they had achieved their own freedom, in other words, once they owned and controlled the means of production, Marx predicted that historical change would come to an end, that the dialectic would cease. There would no longer be any opposing interests to give rise to an antithesis or a new synthesis. The end of history, the goal of history for Marx, would be the achievement of freedom for the workers of the world. Everyone would have freedom, and no one would be under the control of anyone else.

While Marx's ideas of historical change and history's eventual outcome remain very appealing to the have-nots of this world, his predictions have not proved to be very accurate. Because of the complexity of human nature and human social arrangements, it is doubtful that once the workers control their own destiny, conflict will cease. Since Marx wrote, workers have failed to regard themselves as a united group. They have developed distinctions among themselves, such as who is unionized, who is skilled, who is a foreman, who is foreign-born. So even among workers themselves, the distinction between haves and have-nots continues.

It can be argued that the very distinction between haves and have-nots is oversimplified. Marx used that distinction as was shown to describe the classes, or social groupings of people, found in any given society. However, when sociologists, who study society, have looked at these groupings, they have had to develop many more categories than Marx anticipated. People are placed in the upper upper class, the upper class, the upper middle class, the middle class, the lower middle class, etc., to offer just one example. When sociologists attempt to organize society into categories of classes, they cannot depend entirely on ownership of the means of production. They have had to look at education, ratings by other people, family background, lifestyle, and activities as well as income and occupation. Would a college professor who comes from a historically prominent but no longer wealthy family, who earns a modest salary and lives in university housing with his wife and children be considered upper class or middle class?

It would appear that even Marx recognized some of these difficulties. When he applied his categories to the nineteenth-century upheavals in France, for example, he came up against small shopkeepers who certainly weren't the owners of the means of production, nor were they workers. However, Marx did not abandon his have–have-not classification scheme and tended to treat this particular group as dependents or tools of the owners of the means of production. Whether that was an accurate description is open to debate.

The notion of opposing interests, of conflicting views of the haves and have-nots as the moving force of historical change is very attractive. It provides a simple way to interpret events and to find heroes and villains. Perhaps that is why Marx's view of history has become so popular, especially among the poorer peoples of this planet. They can easily apply Marx's idea of economic determinism, particularly his concern with the ownership of the means of production, to their own situations.

The leaders of an impoverished, underdeveloped country, such as Nicaragua, can use Marx's ideas to explain why their nation has lagged so far behind industrialized states. They can claim that Nicaragua's means of production have been for many years under the control of foreign nations, like the United States. The leaders can also point to foreign investors and corporations, like the United Fruit Company, who used the country's resources and labor for their own benefit. They can claim that Nicaragua has been exploited by those who controlled its economy for selfish interests, and that is why the economy of the country is now so backward and underdeveloped.

It is an argument that people can grasp quickly because it is simplistic. It is a single-factor argument, that is, an argument based on one condition and only one condition. It ignores the complexities of a total situation. To blame economic conditions, or more specifically those who own the means of production, for all the historical ills of a nation or even the supposed shortcomings of individuals and groups is to ignore other contributing factors which may be equally important.

In the case of Nicaragua, other factors that may have played an important role in the country's lack of development include a high birth rate, a high rate of illiteracy, insufficient diet, a history of unstable government, uneven population settlements, high rates of disease, and even devastating earthquakes.

Members of the working class can find Marx's doctrines appealing, too. If steelworkers were to apply Marx's argument, they might look at the boss's expensive car and chauffeur, his private estate, his vacations abroad, his well-groomed appearance and claim that the boss has all those advantages because he owns the steel mill. According to steelworkers, the boss doesn't have to work for his living; he doesn't have to live on low wages and try hard to make ends meet. Yet, there have been factory workers with little take-home pay who have risen to become the heads of large companies, for example, Andrew Carnegie and United States Steel. People can sometimes make their own opportunities. They are not, as Marx's theory would necessarily have us believe, simply victims of their economic circumstances.

Individuals can also be tempted to adopt Marxist explanations. When a teacher gives a math test and a rich student does well while a needy student does poorly, it is easy to say, and it sometimes is correct to say, that the rich student did well because he or she had the advantages of wealth. Those advantages might include a family that valued learning and equipment such as a desk and books. On the other hand, such an interpretation of the two students' grades might be very misleading. It is also possible to argue that the rich student happened to be smarter in math, but that same student might be weaker in another subject, say English. It is also possible to argue that the rich student studied harder for the test while the poorer student goofed off and went out with friends. Once again, individual effort might prove more crucial to success than material conditions.

So in looking at the method Marx used to analyze historical change and the conclusions he reached as to the final goal of history, it is important to be objective. While Marx's arguments may appear attractive, easily understood, and relevant everywhere, his analysis as well as his predictions may indeed be faulty. To attempt to apply the scientific method to history and society is a commendable effort, but the subject matter is so complex and Marx's knowledge of science was so primitive and oversimplified that on balance, despite the popularity of his conclusions, they must indeed be questioned and held suspect. With that caution in mind, Marx's ideas can be probed further. Since the workers had a special role to play in reaching the ultimate goal of all history, Marx's discussion of their situation and their special destiny must be examined in greater detail.

CHAPTER SIX
WORKERS AS VICTIMS

From his studies, Marx predicted that as history progressed, the working class would have a special role to play in the destiny of humankind. With the unfolding of the dialectic, the workers would inevitably attain power, creating a new synthesis in which capitalists could no longer oppress them. In the absence of oppression, all class struggle would cease. It is important to look at the way Marx described the workers as well as the work they did in order to understand why he singled out the workers for such an important part in historical change, how they would bring that change about, and what would happen after that change.

For Marx, the workers were an oppressed economic class within industrial societies. In making this claim, he was not referring only to the long hours that men, women, and children labored in factories, the low wages they received, their squalid living conditions, or the shortness of their lives. He was concerned with the total injustice of their situation. Workers were the most numerous group in industrial societies and yet they were treated the worst; they were exploited, used for the benefit of others. He referred to these exploited workers as the proletariat, a term ancient Romans used to describe the propertyless classes. Marx labeled their middle-class employers who owned the means of production the bourgeoisie, a French word that was associated with the qualities of pettyness and a preoccupation with material things. He called the economic system in which the bourgeoisie exploited the proletariat for their own profit the capitalist system. Most economists describe a capitalist economy as one in which private individuals or corporations own the means of producing, distributing, and selling goods and services.

Marx was most concerned with the plight of the people he called the proletariat. He depicted them as outcasts in their own countries. They were isolated from each other by the long hours they labored, their families were broken up by the shifts each member worked, and they were even separated from the results of their long efforts, from the products they produced. They were left alone, cast adrift in a society that had little concern for their welfare. Therefore, Marx insisted that the workers owed no loyalty to bourgeois institutions or systems of government. They had been thrust outside the system. They should have no ties to nation or state. As a perpetual exile who had found refuge in England, Marx had little respect for nationalist loyalties, so why should the workers, exiled within their own countries? The term alienation defines this total sense of loneliness, meaninglessness, and separation that Marx was describing.

In Marx's time, the prevailing attitude in capitalist society was one of *laissez-faire*, letting people do for themselves without outside intervention. It was assumed that if everyone pursued his or her own interests and did not interfere with one another's enterprises, all would turn out well. Furthermore, in Marx's later years, a movement known as Social Darwinism became popular. It applied the evolutionary theories of Charles Darwin to human society and claimed that the process of natural selection would ensure that only the fittest in society survived. If the working classes failed to survive the miserable conditions of their existence, they would be doing society a service. It would disturb the order of things to intervene on their behalf. For example, there were no entitlement programs to give food stamps or medical care to the needy. Workers were left to fend for themselves. Only gradually did governments and private charitable groups begin to recognize that laws had to be passed and efforts made to remedy some of the worst abuses of the laissez-faire economy and Social Darwinist indifference.

In Marx's view, alienation extended into the social relations among people. More and more, these relationships were based on a cash nexus, or monetary bond. The relationships became very impersonal. For example, when people sat down at a restaurant to eat, when they went to the post office to mail a letter, when they went to a store to buy food, they were no longer concerned with the waiter or waitress, the postal clerk, or the storekeeper as individuals with their own personal interests or lives. People no longer cared or were concerned if the waiter had a headache, if the postal clerk just moved to a new home, if the storekeeper became a grandparent for the first time. What mattered was that the waiter took the order and brought the food, that the postal clerk accepted the letter and put it in the right bin, or that the storekeeper had fresh produce. The relationships focused on the exchange of goods and services for money. Anything else no longer mattered.

Under these conditions, the proletariat could derive little pleasure or satisfaction from their daily lives. When they turned to religious institutions for comfort, they were told to be patient and await the blessings of an afterlife. The churches at that time were not concerned with the workers' problems. Marx claimed that this lack of concern proved his point that the owners of the means of production controlled the major institutions of society and used them to keep themselves in power. They used the churches to keep the lower class submissive and obedient. After all, church officials were often members of important families. They would be determined to keep things just as they were.

These observations led Marx to issue his famous remark that religion "is the opium of the people." Religion, like opium, he believed, would keep the mind dulled and accepting. If the proletariat were repeatedly told that an afterlife was their reward for their sufferings on earth, they would be discouraged from protesting the miserable conditions they endured. They would stay in their place, humbly accepting their lot. Bruno Bauer's teaching at the University of Berlin had left its mark on Karl Marx.

This sense of alienation Marx had described so poignantly transferred over to the workplace as well. Marx noted that in earlier times, skilled craftsmen labored together in small, friendly workshops where they developed close ties to one another. They made a product with their own hands and tools and then sold it directly to an appreciative customer.

He lamented that in his day workers were becoming no more than cogs in the vast machines they tended. Marx wrote, "The work of the proletarians has lost all individual character and, consequently, all charm for the workman. He has become an appendage to the machine." No longer did workers proudly make a completed product, such as a pair of shoes. Rather, they produced a part, a piece of the shoe, such as a last or a sole. What's more, their work was sold by others. They did not sell the shoes directly to the customer. Instead, the owner of the shoe factory would hire salespeople to perform that task. So the proletariat was isolated from the satisfaction of seeing the completed product and from the reaction of the consumer who purchased it. From Marx's perspective, this type of alienation was deplorable.

Studying these working conditions from an economic perspective, Marx concluded that workers were being cheated out of the fruits of their labor, a most important form of alienation. Marx found this economic alienation to be so unjust that he felt certain it would give rise to serious opposition. Then the dialectic would advance, historical change would occur, and humanity would have arrived at its ultimate goal.

Marx's explanation of how the proletariat was cheated by the bourgeoisie involves a complicated discussion of economics. He went back to a tradition over two hundred years old, including such notable theorists as John Locke, to resurrect the labor theory of value. He simply took this theory for granted and never bothered to prove it. Simply put, the theory holds that how much a good or service is worth depends *solely* upon the amount of labor that goes into making it or doing it. Obviously there are many different goods and services for sale in a marketplace. How are their worth, their value, to be measured? How can they be compared to one another when, for example, shoes are so different from soap?

According to Marx, the way to assign values to these different products is to determine the amount of labor they require. It is the labor spent on production that counts and not the raw materials, the equipment used to make it, or any other factor that determines what a product is worth. Capital, from this point of view, is merely regarded as stored-up past labor. According to this theory, there should be no profits, or funds gained from the difference between the costs of making a product and the amount a customer pays for it. The customer should simply pay the value of the labor and the materials used.

Marx was arguing that ideally in a society, workers should produce the goods and services needed to satisfy the community's wants, not to satisfy the bourgeoisie's needs for profits!

Modern economists find the labor theory of value unacceptable. Even economists of Marx's day had rejected the labor theory of value, because they recognized that there were other factors as well that determined the value of a product. One of those factors is capital, which includes assets such as materials, tools, equipment, and plant space. They made room in their theories for profits as well since they believed that the private owners of the means of production, the capitalists, made a useful contribution to the economy in amassing the funds to start business enterprises, which could involve considerable risk if a new product or service was involved, and in managing those enterprises and keeping them financially sound.

Marx certainly recognized that the bourgeoisie, or capitalists, made profits, but he denounced these gains, arguing that they were based on the exploitation of workers. To support his position, Marx grafted onto the labor theory of value an original contribution of his own, the theory of surplus value. This theory holds that when workers make goods to be sold to consumers, they are not paid the full value of what they make. In other words, they are not paid for the full amount of labor they have put into the product they made.

What they are paid is subsistence wages, a sum just sufficient to keep them alive and working. Marx borrowed this idea, known as the iron law of wages. It implied that workers would always be condemned to earn the barest minimum. However, this "law" fast became unpopular because in fact, by 1850 the wages of workers did rise. Nonetheless, Marx claimed that the proletariat was paid subsistence wages because their employers paid them for the value of their labor power, their capacity to make things. According to Marx, workers were not paid for the value of their labor, or what they produced. Workers had to sell their labor power to employers as if the workers themselves were goods or services for sale and thereby transformed themselves from human beings into commodities, or items offered for sale, a terrible form of alienation.

The difference between the workers' labor power and the labor value of the goods they made was surplus value. In other words, the difference between what the product was worth in terms of the amount of labor put into it and the amount of wages a worker received was surplus value. If a worker produced two pairs of shoes worth ten dollars each when they were sold and received the equivalent of two dollars a day for making them, the surplus value amounted to eight dollars. Surplus value was the profit those who owned the means of production and paid the workers gained. However, from Marx's point of view, these owners, the bourgeoisie, did not deserve their profits, since they contributed no labor to the productive process, and labor, for Marx, was the only source of value. Ideally, the workers should have received the full ten dollars!

Since the workers were denied the full value of what they produced, and were instead paid subsistence wages, the economic system would be constantly troubled by the overproduction of goods that people could not afford to buy. Marx believed that the owners of the means of production would constantly have to produce more and more in order to make money. He felt that if they cut back on production and laid off workers, they would eventually be wiped out.

Marx also thought that if the bourgeoisie bought new equipment to increase production and compete successfully with other owners, they would necessarily make the proletariat work longer to accumulate more surplus value in order to pay for the expensive equipment. Evidently, Marx did not see machinery as labor-saving devices. How surprised he might be at the robot-operated equipment in modern factories! Furthermore, Marx insisted that as new machinery was introduced into factories, more and more workers would lose their jobs, a condition now known as technological unemployment. The record on this prediction has been mixed. Indeed some jobs have been lost when industries became obsolete. For example, the invention of the automobile certainly reduced the number of blacksmiths as well as the number of people involved in making horse-drawn buggies and carriages. Yet, it opened new opportunities in car manufacture and highway construction, to say nothing of the whole gasoline industry and roadside restaurants and stores.

Marx blamed low wages and overproduction for the troubles economic systems of his day experienced. He claimed that since capitalists constantly sought profits, they were forced to produce more and more. Since they could not afford to control or curtail production, they would always have to keep wages low and search for new markets for their goods.

National economies in Marx's day did indeed suffer periodic booms and busts, or cycles of rising prices, greater production, and higher employment followed by falling prices, reduced output, and unemployment. Modern economists as well have linked the ups and downs of the business cycle to factors such as overproduction of goods and lack of buyer purchasing power. However, they have recognized the interplay of many other contributing factors. Moreover, since Marx's time, capitalist governments have taken steps to try to control the excesses of the cycle. The actions of the Federal Reserve System in the United States to increase or limit the money supply is just one example of this kind of government intervention. In addition, there is a whole network of government programs to assist the unemployed.

Poor working conditions, low wages, technological unemployment, overproduction, and the effects of periodic booms and busts were just some of the injustices and flaws Marx found in the capitalist economic system. He often referred to them as contradictions, contrary developments within the same setting, which would cause the dialectic to advance. A central contradiction he discovered was that the capitalist economy created a means of producing enough goods and services to satisfy societal wants, but on the other hand, the capitalist system, limited by the search for profits and the private ownership of productive capacity, distributed those goods and services unevenly so that the needs of the few were satisfied but the needs of the many went unfulfilled. Marx expected that this fundamental contradiction between production and distribution would bring about the rise of a new economic system as the dialectic unfolded. The contradictions of bourgeois economics were discussed at great length in Marx's three-volume work *Capital*.

In this work as well as in other writings, Marx took capitalist society to task. Yet within the framework of dialectical materialism, he did recognize that in the past members of the bourgeoisie had many achievements to their credit. He noted that they brought an end to feudal society, destroying the bonds that bound the exploited class to the land and to their aristocratic superiors. Marx credits the bourgeoisie for their voyages of discovery, opening up the New World; the rise of cities; the extension of civilization to primitive peoples; the rise of internationalism in trade and in the arts and literature; increased productivity; as well as improvements in transportation and communication. Those accomplishments, however, took place in the past.

Marx condemned the bourgeoisie for the new miseries they inflicted on humankind since they came to power. He insisted that their much praised concept of self-government with its representative institutions was merely a method of managing capitalists' affairs, not those of the proletariat, which was kept from participation or power.

Bourgeois notions of freedom, according to Marx, meant simply the freedom to exploit others. For example, what did freedom of religion mean if all religions preached a doctrine of submission to capitalist employers? What did free speech mean if the owners of newspapers were the reigning bourgeoisie? He felt that free trade—the right to exchange goods without government interference in the form of taxes, or customs duties, or other obstacles such as quotas—was a mere disguise for the capitalists' need to constantly expand their markets. What protection did hapless people have against a glut of unwanted foreign goods? What benefits did workers receive if free trade meant freedom from government inspection and regulation of conditions of employment to enrich the bourgeoisie? As was seen earlier, Marx also accused the bourgeoisie of reducing professional and family relationships to monetary ties.

As a keen observer of events, Marx could not fail to notice rising wages, the rise of labor unions, and by 1870 or so the right of workers to vote. With higher wages, the workers would have more money to improve the quality of their lives. Labor unions would allow workers to negotiate for wages and conditions of employment with their employers on a group basis rather than individually. That way they would have more power to press for change. An individual employee could be fired for demanding a decent wage, but concerted demands by a union were less likely to be ignored. As soon as the workers could vote, they began to form workers' political parties. These would introduce legislation to improve the lot of the proletariat. In doing so, they were working within the capitalist system that Marx had condemned. How was Marx to reconcile these improvements in the material conditions of the workers' lives with his theories of capitalism and its mistreatment of the proletariat?

Marx tended to condemn these developments as opportunism. Workers were taking advantage of the capitalist system to further their own ends, but Marx felt that such gains as they achieved could only be temporary. They would never be able to change the whole system by accepting the reforms it condescended to offer them. However, they would be training themselves in the uses of power, training they would eventually put to good use.

Marx had singled out the proletariat to play an important role in historical change, and he wasn't about to abandon this position no matter how much better off the workers became. He still maintained that the proletariat owed no loyalty to capitalist institutions or governments. That is why he urged: "The proletarians have nothing to lose but their chains. They have a world to win. Workingmen of all countries, unite!" The proletariat had a mission decreed by the dialectic and confirmed by economic determinism. They were going to take over the capitalist system and run the economy for the benefit of all humankind. Exploitation would come to an end.

CHAPTER SEVEN
REVOLUTION
AS A SOLUTION

Marx predicted that the proletariat eventually would gain control of the capitalist economy. It would use the instruments of production to bring to an end the exploitation of workers by employers and satisfy the needs of all members of society. In doing so, it would be fulfilling a historic mission.

How Marx intended this to be accomplished is not altogether clear. Would the workers come to power gradually, working within the system to bring about its destruction as the dialectic unfolded, or would they use force and violence to seize the means of production from the bourgeoisie and gain control of the state? The former, gradual approach to change could be called evolutionary while the latter, more aggressive approach to change could be seen as revolutionary. Arguments on behalf of both positions can be found in Marx's writings, although the revolutionary side of Marx is more frequently associated with his doctrines.

The evolutionary side of Marx's thoughts takes its logic from the concept of dialectical materialism. Citing passages from Marx's *Capital,* Engels and other Marxists pointed out how the contradictions in the capitalist economy Marx had described would eventually bring about its downfall. Marx and his followers argued that the downswings of the business cycle would bring production to a standstill as markets became glutted with goods no one could afford to buy. These recessions or depressions would wipe out small, less profitable firms, increasing the ranks of the proletariat as more and more workers became unemployed. They called these unemployed the industrial reserve army. Bankrupt capitalists, whether the former owners of factories or small shopkeepers, would join their ranks, increasing the number of paupers in a society.

Companies would merge, seeking to control entire industries. Marx himself argued that as capitalism matured, ruthless competition for profits between bourgeois owners of the means of production would gradually reduce their numbers and cause the more successful to consolidate their holdings. Competition would be replaced by monopoly, where one large company, or trust, controls the entire market for a good or service. Marx anticipated that the state would eventually take over these trusts, with salaried employees performing the functions of management.

The capitalists would no longer be performing any useful function at all. They would become farther and farther removed from productive activities. The process of consolidation resulting in state-run corporations would prove just how unnecessary and useless the bourgeoisie were as a class.

By using the political process—by voting, forming parties, winning elections, and running governments—the workers could take control of the huge state-run factories and plants. Then they would have the power to bring about needed changes in the purposes and functions of production. Worker-run organizations would seek to satisfy human needs, not to make profits. Marx himself urged the proletariat to strive to bring about democratic governments. This is the kind of tactic he used in Cologne, Germany, during the Revolution of 1848. He felt that through democratic procedures, the proletariat could take control of their countries to effect needed changes. The changes would come about gradually, but they would be inevitable. For the most part, the dialectic would unfold peacefully.

This evolutionary account suggests that changes in the material conditions of production would inevitably occur and that the workers would gradually assume control. It contrasts sharply with the revolutionary side of Marx's writing, which advocated the need for more violent seizures of power. Marx justified the use of force to overthrow bourgeois regimes on several grounds.

First of all, he maintained that capitalist systems were so entrenched, so firmly established, that it would take violence, similar to that of the French Revolution of 1789, to bring about their downfall. Not only did the capitalists own the means of production, they controlled the government, armed forces, transportation, and communications, to name just a few of the societal institutions under bourgeois power. The proletariat had to take over the productive forces of the society, but in doing so, they would have to seize the other institutions of society as well. In doing so, they would be changing the whole way of life in their societies. Since material conditions determined the way in which people lived, the proletariat takeover would in effect uproot and alter the entire bourgeois culture. The forces of production did not exist in a vacuum.

A second reason why this revolution would be violent was that the bourgeoisie were not going to sit back passively and accept proletarian rule. Marx held that historically, the ruling classes never surrendered power without fighting and supported his position with examples from the feudal era and the period of absolute monarchies. Marx fully expected that the bourgeoisie would resist the proletarian movement with military forces and weapons, thereby forcing the proletariat to defend itself in similar fashion. The proletariat was more numerous, but the bourgeoisie would be better trained and better supplied. So the fighting might be severe.

Marx saw himself as a revolutionary, and today his doctrines are very much associated with revolution. It is helpful to remember that the word *revolution* has more than one meaning. When used to describe the motion of the earth around the sun or the wheel on an axle, it refers to a sense of turning around. Applied to human behavior, the notion of turning around suggests change, the introduction of something new, a novelty. In this sense of the word, revolution takes on the meaning of discarding the old and bringing about a total change. By mechanizing the way things were made with the advent of the steam engine, electricity, and factories, the rise of mass production has been labeled the *Industrial Revolution*. It certainly changed the way people lived.

In other words, a revolution need not necessarily involve bloodshed and violence even though it may be associated with great social upheavals and dislocations. Since Marx was advocating social and economic changes that were radically new, he should be regarded as a revolutionary independently of the issue of whether his writings preached gradual or abrupt methods of bringing those changes about and whether or not at varied times in his life he acted to support revolutionary violence or to foster compromise with reform movements.

Whether the change took place peacefully and gradually or violently and abruptly, Marx felt that it could not occur until the material conditions for a proletarian takeover had been met. He sketched out these requirements in some detail. For revolution to take place, the society would have to be highly industrialized. Marx expected revolutionary change to come about first in the most advanced industrial nations because they would have a large class of exploited workers. He specifically denied that a proletarian revolution could arise, let alone succeed, in a backward, semi-industrialized, agricultural country where most of the population were peasants or farmers. For Marx, revolution was an urban, not a rural, phenomenon.

Marx's acute recognition of the importance of material conditions to the success of a revolutionary effort led him to conclude that Russia was too backward a nation, too underindustrialized, to conduct a successful proletarian revolution. He did argue that Russia was ripe for a revolution that would wipe out the last vestiges of absolute monarchy. History, of course, has demonstrated how wrong Marx's prediction was, because a proletarian revolution did succeed in that underindustrialized absolute monarchy.

A second prerequisite for revolution was that capitalistic competition would have to have reached the stage where ownership of the means of production was concentrated in the hands of a very small group. Former members of the bourgeoisie having competed and lost would join the growing ranks of the proletariat. Of course, it is easier to triumph over one's enemies when there are fewer of them.

While competition has in fact reduced the number of corporations in many industries, at the same time, ownership of those companies has diversified. Today, many workers own shares in business companies which entitle them to vote for the managers who run the businesses. What's more, the ranks of the middle class have increased as workers have become more prosperous.

Third, the proletariat would have had to develop class consciousness, an awareness of its overwhelming common identity and interest as a class, as well as a sense of its historic mission. This is why Marx worked so hard for the success of the First International. Workers' identity as a class would have to become so strong that it would transcend national loyalties, which were loyalties to capitalist societies anyway. Marx fully expected the workers to develop a sense of international solidarity with one another. Their common interest as workers would be extended to include the exploited proletariat worldwide. They would be ready and eager to overthrow the petty, nationalist, capitalist governments that kept them divided by country and oppressed.

What common interests workers did have were instead channeled into their support for unions and for political parties, to "bread and butter issues," matters of wages, hours, and working conditions, issues that would improve their lives rather than overturn the system in which those lives were spent. The nationalistic loyalties of workers during World War I and World War II, to give just two examples, never came into question. British workers fought both times against their German counterparts, and few on either side gave a thought to their common interests as oppressed members of the proletariat.

During his lifetime, Marx tried to apply his theory of revolution. He attempted to assess how far the proletariat had come in attaining their historic goal, to trace the stages of a potential revolutionary outbreak, and to determine which of the countries of his day were ready for revolution. He examined the material conditions of the past and of his age as signposts pointing to revolution, to try to estimate how many of the needed prerequisites of revolution had been met. However, Marx the prophet of revolution was constantly at odds with Marx the observant journalist. Despite the prophet's optimistic interpretations of events and predictions of success, the more realistic journalist recognized that the revolution had to be constantly postponed.

To assess how far the proletariat had come in developing an awareness of its common interests as a class and its historic mission, Marx looked to the past. He noted that when the factory system first developed, individual workers might attack the instruments of production rather than the owners of that equipment. They engaged in isolated acts of sabotage to express their dissatisfaction. Since they did not yet recognize that the bourgeoisie, not machinery, was their enemy, they were still willing to fight the bourgeoisie's battles against precapitalist, reactionary sectors of society, such as absolute monarchists and landowners.

As industrialization developed, machinery eliminated distinctions between different kinds of labor, and the working class grew more numerous. Workers began to recognize their common needs and formed unions to keep their wages from falling further. The cause of unionism was helped by improvements in the means of communication, which allowed more and more workers to join together to promote their common interests.

Here, Marx was merely interpreting events that had already taken place. Although he anticipated that occasional riots might result from union activities, he did not mistake them for revolutionary activities. He predicted that the fruits of these skirmishes would be short-lived, but he hoped that these local struggles would make workers aware of their common plight and foster in them a consciousness of their mutual interests, their class interests. He did not expect that any concession the workers won from the bourgeoisie would be lasting or would truly improve the workers' lot.

He also claimed that members of the bourgeoisie, whose drive for profits put them in competition with the bourgeoisie in foreign countries, would enlist the support of the proletariat in the political affairs of the day. In this way, the bourgeoisie would help to educate the proletariat. He appeared to be explaining why, instead of overthrowing the capitalist system, workers were agreeable to working within it for improvements in their lives. He was coming to terms with the fact that workers were voting and in other ways participating in capitalist political systems. The inclusion of the proletariat in bourgeois politics also helped him account for the fact that the benefits the workers were able to achieve fostered their national loyalties, rather than a sense of international identification with an oppressed proletariat. It would explain their willingness to fight in capitalist armies. To some extent workers did develop a class consciousness, an important prerequisite of revolution for Marx, but, as was mentioned earlier, it never replaced their sense of patriotism the way he had hoped it would.

Marx had indeed expected the class struggle to intensify. At its peak, he even expected that some sectors of the ruling class would join forces with the proletariat, just as some French nobles had sided with the revolutionaries in 1789. He also anticipated that to save themselves from extinction, conservative groups such as peasants, shopkeepers, and artisans would join the fight against the bourgeoisie, whose competitive industries were destroying their way of life. This did not occur in the industrialized nations he had studied. Instead, such class consciousness as did develop led these threatened groups to identify their interests even more closely with the middle class, or capitalist, sector of society. However, the pattern Marx outlined was duplicated in some of the Marxist revolutions that finally occurred during the twentieth century.

To trace the stages of a revolutionary outbreak, Marx relied on his reading of history. At first, the struggle of the proletariat against the bourgeoisie would be a scattered, random, local effort. Then it would involve an entire nation. Eventually it would spread beyond national borders to other industrial countries, much as capitalism replaced feudalism. The Russian Revolution, which brought the Soviet regime into being, started as a series of local uprisings. After the Soviet leadership gained control of all of Russia and secured its power against internal uprisings and foreign invasion, it did, indeed, go on to spawn Marxist revolutions in other nations.

At different points in his lifetime, Marx did believe that there were certain industrial countries actually ripe for a proletarian revolution. While he shifted his specific targets as the twists and turns of current events dictated, he did claim as the occasion demanded that Germany, England, and lastly France were possibly ripe for a proletarian revolution. As France experienced various upheavals from 1848 to 1871, Marx's hopes rose and fell. When workers, among others, formed the Paris Commune for a short time in 1871 to attempt to impose a radical republican government on the French provinces in the wake of France's defeat during the Franco-Prussian War, Marx was briefly encouraged. However, savage fighting between the *Communards* and the forces of the existing republican government led to the destruction of the Commune. Marx saw this as a setback for the French proletariat and no longer expected it to serve as the forefront of a workers' revolution.

The lesson Marx derived from this historical episode as well as from the earlier turmoil of 1848 was that material conditions must ripen before a national, no less a world, proletarian revolution could succeed. These unsuccessful attempts, however, were not without value. They were signposts on the road to ultimate success. They served to increase the workers' awareness of their group interests, of their exploitation at the hands of the bourgeoisie, of their ultimate destiny. Marx's interpretation of the current events of his day possibly confused the desirable with the possible. At times, Marx the prophet of revolution tried to ignore Marx the veteran journalist. Despite evidence to the contrary, he continued to predict that as workers developed a class consciousness, they would recognize that they had a destiny to overthrow the capitalist system.

The all-determining role that Marx assigned to material conditions raises interesting questions about the leadership of revolutionary movements. What factors contribute most to successful leadership, personal attributes or the course of events? Should the leadership of the proletariat be drawn exclusively from the working class? What is the relationship between the leaders and the led? When can revolutionary leaders take action to overthrow the capitalist system?

According to Marx, leaders can only be the products of their times. No matter how talented or capable individual leaders are, their leadership will fail if they try to move against the currents of history. Only if material conditions can support a revolution, will leaders of revolutionary movements succeed. In this way Marx attempted to resolve a timeless issue: do great leaders make history or does history make great leaders? From Marx's standpoint, a Washington, a Napoleon, or even a Lenin or Mao Tse-tung could succeed only if he moved in the same direction as the dialectical forces that caused the revolution he eventually led.

Marx never abandoned his belief in the importance of economic circumstances to human endeavors. Thus he reminded the leadership of the proletarian movement that it could not afford to ignore the material prerequisites of revolution that Marx had outlined, no matter how dedicated it was to revolution. This was the lesson he learned in 1848 when he quarreled with his more hotheaded colleagues who rushed in to fight prematurely.

Marx referred to the people who understood the historic mission of the working class and endeavored to bring it about as the vanguard of the proletariat. Marx did not insist that the leadership come from the working class; he could not object to its recruitment from outside, for example, from intellectuals. If he had, he would have had trouble justifying his own role. What he did insist upon is that the leadership not form a separate, elitist clique of its own. He urged them to work with all workers' parties in every country where they existed. He felt that these leaders should serve to make the proletariat more aware of its common interests as a class, to point out the international bonds that drew workers together, and to constantly keep the goal of revolution in mind, even if that revolution had to await the future.

Perhaps people could not make such events as a proletarian revolution happen by wishful thinking and conspiratorial plotting—what Marx would call subjective conditions—but they could be on the lookout for the objective conditions—those material circumstances that would cause that revolution to occur. When these existed, the workers could finally take action. However, to the frustration of Marx's followers, he never provided a timetable of revolution. Did a revolution have to await the spontaneous uprising of the proletariat or could its leaders take action when they felt conditions to be ripe and expect the proletariat to follow them? This question was to plague Marx's successors, especially Lenin, who tried to apply Marx's doctrine of revolution to Russia. Marx could demonstrate why a revolution was necessary. He could even describe the material conditions necessary to create a context favorable to revolution, but in predicting the course of human history, he could not be specific. He could not state precisely how, when, and where a revolution of the proletariat should take place. His was a portrait, not a blueprint.

However vague Marx's plans for revolution were, the vision of the future he held out to his followers was even more sketchy. He promised that after a revolution succeeded, people would no longer be bound by material circumstances. Only then would they be truly free to follow their individual destinies. To see what Marx meant and how his goals would be accomplished, it is important to examine the results of a successful proletarian revolution as Marx described it.

CHAPTER EIGHT
A VISION OF THE FUTURE

At the conclusion of a proletarian revolution, Marx expected bourgeois society and all of its institutions to be replaced by a classless society, a communist society. In such a social setting, humankind would finally be set free from the artificially imposed scarcity and want of capitalism, with its ruthless pursuit of profit and its code of selfishness. People would be able to truly fulfill their potential. However, Marx well recognized that after decades of capitalism, the uprooting of bourgeois institutions could not take place overnight. It would be unrealistic to expect that society would change just by waving a magic wand. For this reason, Marx anticipated that a transitional period would be necessary. He called the period raw communism.

During this phase, Marx expected great dislocations and enormous upsets. He knew that this would be a difficult time for people. They would have to unlearn all the bourgeois ways of thinking and doing things that had become an integral part of their lives. Initially this readjustment process could be quite painful and confusing.

Yet, the goal of this suffering would make it worthwhile.

Marx urged that all private property be abolished. He reasoned that if the material conditions of self-interest and the profit motive disappeared, the reason for perpetuating class distinctions and exploitation would also disappear. If people no longer owned property, if they could no longer distinguish between what belonged to them and what belonged to someone else, they would not be able to control others. No one would be any more powerful than anyone else. This would encourage the development of common bonds and feelings of mutual concern and caring. It would make the classless society of Marx's predictions a reality.

Marx insisted that the traditional bourgeois family be broken up and replaced by free relationships between members of both sexes. He seemed to be eliminating any private or personal ties that would form competing loyalties to set people against each other. He held that the bourgeois family was a sham anyway since the relationships among its members were purely economic, while the proletarian family with its long hours of hard labor was a mere fiction. Many of his mid-Victorian, nineteenth-century readers found this proposal scandalous. Of course, people's living arrangements are somewhat more flexible today, and it can be argued that the traditional family of husband, wife, and children living under one roof and rearing their offspring to maturity is slowly being replaced by single-parent households, as well as other groupings of adults and children that may be less permanent in nature.

Marx's plans also included having the proletariat run the factories in a cooperative rather than exploitative spirit. He offered few specifics as to how this could be done. He simply compared the concerted activities of the workers with those of a symphony orchestra. In this way, he meant to show that individual artists, such as violinists, flutists, and drummers, would combine their special talents to bring to life a concerto or a symphony. By making the comparison between a factory and an orchestra, Marx seemed to be suggesting that skilled workers were artists who could give life to well-crafted objects. In the absence of capitalistic exploitation, their work would become just as creative as that of musicians.

Marx was certainly aware that orchestras are led by conductors, who bring the efforts of the various musicians into harmony. He allowed that the factory would require a director, who would perform his function much like that of a symphony conductor. Factory operations, like those in an orchestra, seem to require the discipline of leadership. Yet Marx did not wish to encourage ranks and orders within the emerging classless society. Was Marx contradicting himself? Perhaps, perhaps not. If the leadership were guided by the wishes of the led, then the power it exercised would be limited and acceptable to all. What Marx seemed to forget is that some symphony conductors are very exacting and demanding people. These conductors tend to dominate their musicians in order to have their playing reflect the conductors' ideas of what a particular piece should sound like, not the individual orchestra members' ideas. What guarantee was there that a factory director might not behave in a similar fashion? Such leadership may actually be necessary. A symphony might sound strange indeed if the violinists chose to emphasize the role of the violin section while the drummers felt that their part was more important and sought to drown out the other orchestra members. Similarly, a coat might prove impossible to wear if the workers making the buttons had one idea of what size to make while the workers making buttonholes had another size in mind. Who would resolve their disagreements and by what method?

Marx also expected population resettlements to eliminate urban-rural distinctions among people. Once again, he failed to provide concrete suggestions as to how this might be accomplished. Would people be asked to volunteer to move? Would they be forced to relocate? When Moslems and Hindus were partitioned in 1947 and Pakistan was created out of parts of India, many people were required to resettle. The results were often bloody and violent. Would the redistribution of population counteract the allure of city life, which drew rural folk from the hardship and monotony of the farm to the squalid conditions of slums and factories in Marx's day? Or would the entire countryside gradually become urbanized?

Marx went so far as to design a provisional program of action for the period of raw communism. He presented it as a general plan to be adapted to the needs of the varied countries where it was to be applied. Some of the plan merely repeated the measures just mentioned, but some of it went farther. In the *Communist Manifesto*, Marx listed his requirements:

1. Abolition of property in land and application of all rents of land to public purposes.
2. A heavy progressive or graduated income tax.
3. Abolition of all right of inheritance.
4. Confiscation of all the property of all emigrants and rebels.
5. Centralization of credit in the hands of the State, by means of a national bank with State capital and an exclusive monopoly.
6. Centralization of the means of communication and transport in the hands of the State.
7. Extension of factories and instruments of production owned by the State; the bringing into cultivation of wastelands, and the improvement of the soil generally in accordance with a common plan.

8. Equal liability of all to labor. Establishment of industrial armies, especially for agriculture.
9. Combination of agriculture with manufacturing industries; gradual abolition of the distinction between town and country, by a more equable distribution of the population over the country.
10. Free education for all children in public schools. Abolition of children's factory labor in its present form. Combination of education with industrial production.

Some of Marx's proposals, such as the graduated income tax, state-run transportation systems, the industrialization of agriculture, and free public education, do not appear especially radical from the perspective of the late twentieth century, but at the time that he presented them, they were far from the accepted practices they are today. Others, such as the abolition of private property and a compulsory labor force, seem alien even now.

What is most interesting about Marx's discussion of raw communism is his mention of the state, an institution he tended to describe as an instrument of class oppression. Marx described at great length how aristocrats or the bourgeoisie used the power of the state to keep the workers in their place. If the proletarian revolution succeeded, why wouldn't the workers destroy the state? Why would they need a state?

Marx explained that before a revolution actually took place, as political processes became more democratized, as more and more of the proletariat participated in politics, they would use the state to centralize the instruments of production and wrest capital from the bourgeoisie to start the workers on the road to revolution. After the revolution, the force and power associated with a state would be used to bring about a classless society, to end the exploitation of class by class. Evidently, Marx did not expect the bourgeoisie to become instant proletarians. Despite their dwindling numbers, Marx fully expected the bourgeoisie to cling to and defend its way of life. The continued existence of the state would ensure that they did not succeed, would ensure that the measures Marx proposed were carried out.

Marx called this democratized transitional proletarian state the dictatorship of the proletariat. It would remain in existence during the period of raw communism and then disappear when the material conditions requiring its existence no longer applied. The term *dictatorship* means government by command rather than government by consent. Dictators are known to impose their will upon reluctant subjects. It is somewhat ironic that Marx chose this word to describe the process he expected would liberate humankind from oppression and exploitation. It is even more ironic that the form this dictatorship would take would be democratic rule by the majority, that is, the workers.

When Marx and Engels were asked for details about the structure or function of this dictatorship, they would refer their questioners to the Paris Commune. However, Marx himself recognized that the Paris Commune was merely an isolated and temporary example of workers prematurely attempting to seize power and govern. Marx and Engels used the Commune as a model, but they were not trying to duplicate it in detail.

The term *commune* is intended to summon up images of a close-knit community, of small groups of people cooperating in the management of their common interests. Marx may have chosen this word deliberately, to emphasize the idea that proletarian governments would be collaborative, not selfish enterprises. They would be cooperative, not competitive. This peaceful, consentual description of the communes seems to contrast sharply with the repressive activities associated with the dictatorship of the proletariat. Yet both of these sides of political life are to be found in Marx's account of raw communism.

The features of the Paris Commune that Marx chose

to adapt included a federation, or loose association, of local organizations. These local communes were to be composed of people elected for short terms by universal suffrage, and empowered to administer local affairs. These communes would send delegates to a national organization in Paris. The delegates were bound by formal instructions from their constituents. Marx wanted all public servants, including judges, to be elected to office, an uncommon practice at the time.

Marx expected that the dictatorship of the proletariat would fade away once the transition period was completed. Once the program Marx had formulated was realized, the material conditions of social life would have changed. If there no longer was any private property, there could be no distinction between haves and have-nots. If there were no longer classes, there could no longer be exploitation and thus no need for even the democratic dictatorship that presided over these changes. The forces of dialectical materialism would reach their logical conclusion in the liberation of humankind from greed and from want.

In all of his writings on communist society, Marx took for granted that there would be an abundant supply of goods and services available to everyone. He described this blissful state of affairs with the slogan "From each according to his abilities, to each according to his needs." Marx never took up the question of how the society would be organized to produce what people needed or how what was produced would be distributed to people. He offered one clue when he made a reference to cooperative societies that would produce according to a common plan, but he never developed this notion.

He offered another clue when he wrote that division of labor—that is, parceling out a complicated task into manageable units, each performed by a different person or group—and specialization of function—giving different people with different talents responsibility for a particular task and only that task—dehumanized workers. It restricted them to repetitive activities or roles. For example, a doctor could only be a doctor, not a lawyer or an artist. It limited people's opportunities to be well-rounded, to feel fulfilled. Workers who only produced one part of a shoe day in and day out got little satisfaction from what they did, nor did they have time to develop other interests or new skills.

Marx sets up an ideal of people as "jacks of all trades and masters of none" and condemns the stifling labels of doctor or shoemaker that limit and confine a person to certain activities, and only certain activities. However, people might not shift from job to job as he expected. What's more, some jobs, like that of a doctor, might require long years of training as well as continued practice to keep up the needed skills. The society Marx constructs is one of happy amateurs, but who would want an amateur to operate on him and take out his appendix?

There is little else in his works to explain how this problem of production and distribution would be handled. Marx devoted his attention to freeing people from selfishness and greed, but he never explained how they would maintain themselves after they were liberated from the evil effects of profit-seeking, exploitation, or surplus value.

Marx wished to create an environment in which humankind would no longer be bound by material conditions limiting its creativity and making people the victims of history. At last, they would be free to make of their lives whatever they would and could. With this purpose in mind, Marx was emphatic that the working day be shortened As the twentieth century advanced, his demand was gradually met. However, it raised problems that Marx did not and probably could not anticipate. What would people do with their leisure time? Would they, in fact, use it creatively and constructively? Of course, when people were working fourteen- and then even ten-hour days, returning home exhausted and spent, worrying about spare time was the farthest thing from their minds.

In his attempt to free workers from the demands and monotony of factory life as he knew it, Marx wrote that people would vary the tasks they performed for society. One day they might push a wheelbarrow; another day they might tend work as architects, and then they might return to pushing the wheelbarrow until they were again needed as architects. What this example further suggests is that there would no longer be a societal distinction drawn between those who worked with their brains and those who worked with their hands. All labor would be regarded as equally important and valuable. It would no longer serve as a basis for making some people appear to be better than others. Furthermore, the process of production would become a form of self-fulfillment that people could enjoy at last rather than a dehumanizing necessity of life.

From a twentieth-century perspective, these aims still appear distant and foreign, but Marx can't be faulted for the nobility of his goals. However, it is possible to find a number of practical flaws in Marx's vision of the future, however worthy his intentions were. Aside from the problem of producing and distributing enough goods and services to satisfy members of the society, there are also unsolved problems about how people would perform those functions necessary to keep society going. Aside from the issue of letting amateurs take turns doing tasks, the question must arise as to what would happen if these amateurs individually chose not to change jobs. Marx implied that people would be free to pick and choose what they wanted to do each day. What if everyone decided to push wheelbarrows rather than design or build buildings, if they chose to paint pictures rather than plant potatoes? Why would people want to work? What would happen if some members of Marx's future society were lazy while others were not? What if some were more productive, or more talented, or more gifted than others? Couldn't these distinctions serve as a new basis for dividing people into superior and inferior groupings? Marx's classless society is based on the notion that relationships to the means of production divide people and cause some to feel more valued than others. What if he were wrong? What if there are other more basic divisions among people?

After all the effort Marx made to prove why the coming of socialism was inevitable, his discussion of communist society is anticlimactic. He has surprisingly little to say and what he does say focuses more on the advantages to be gained by humankind than on the specific arrangements that will foster and protect those advantages. He informs his readers about the obstacles that have to be removed for humankind to gain true freedom, but he fails to describe in any detail the structure of the new world facing liberated humankind. What he does say raises more questions than it answers. His brave new world seems quite utopian, an ideal, all-too-perfect vision of the future.

Ironically, Marx and Engels condemned a number of other socialists for being too utopian, for presenting proposals that were based on fantasies and were most impractical. In their writings Marx and Engels took to task the French theorists Charles Fourier (1772–1837) and Henri de Saint-Simon (1760–1825), and the English manufacturer and reformer Robert Owen (1771–1858), among others. Fourier had developed the notion of phalanxes, cooperative agricultural communities, while Saint-Simon advocated a society run by an industrial and scientific elite. Robert Owen established a model factory in New Lanark, Scotland, where he offered his workers decent wages and conditions of employment. He founded several experimental cooperative communities.

Both Marx and Engels recognized that these socialists performed a useful function in criticizing the institutions of bourgeois society. By calling capitalist institutions and practices into question, they helped to arouse the workers' awareness of their class interests. These tracts were indeed educational, but Marx and Engels rejected the constructive proposals these theorists made because they lacked a scientific view of history and therefore failed to recognize the inevitability of a proletarian revolution. These utopians worked within the system, not for its overthrow. Thus from Marx's point of view, they would accomplish little.

As was noted earlier, throughout his life Marx was not especially tolerant of other socialist writers or socialist movements. These individuals or groups might deplore the plight of workers and urge alternative methods of producing and distributing needed goods and services, such as cooperative associations or state-managed factories and warehouses. However, both Marx and Engels felt that these socialists did not go far enough. They accused their colleagues of harboring bourgeois sentiments, of being reluctant to bring about the revolutionary changes needed to completely overhaul capitalist society. By failing to accept the Marxist doctrine of dialectical materialism, they proved themselves to be unscientific. Perhaps this is why Marx apparently called those socialists who followed him communists, those who recognized the need to abolish private property, those who recognized the historic destiny of the proletariat and worked to bring it about.

The quarrels among different socialist movements were to continue long after Marx's death. The scientific theory of socialism that Marx presented to the world was itself subject to differing interpretations as Marx's successors struggled to put his ideas into action. The Marxist movement split into several factions, each maintaining that its version of Marxism was the only true version of Marxism. These differences were to become even more pronounced in the twentieth century.

CHAPTER NINE
MARXISM
AFTER MARX

When Marx died in 1883, the advanced industrial nations of Western Europe were in the midst of rapid social, economic, and political changes. The death rate was falling, as was the birth rate. The size of the population was becoming more stabilized, a pattern typical of developed countries where there are fewer people, but those people live longer and better. The literacy rate, the percentage of people who can read and write, was rising. While compulsory attendance in elementary school had been enacted into law as early as the eighteenth century in Prussia, the heart of what became the German Empire, similar laws were not passed until 1880 in England and 1882 in France. As more and more children were required to attend school, use of child labor began to decline.

As prosperity became more widespread and productivity increased, the nations of western Europe embarked upon a scramble for colonies. The results are sometimes described as imperialism, the control of less developed peoples and territories for purposes of trade, prestige, or security. By 1914, the British had invested an eighth of their national wealth in their colonial empire while the French had invested a tenth of theirs. A fifth of German wealth was placed in foreign investments, but the amount set aside for colonies was small. Germany was a relative latecomer on the colonial scene. Nonetheless, these European powers gained new colonies or trading arrangements almost all over the globe: in Africa, Asia, and the Near East.

These foreign ventures intensified European nationalist rivalries and stirred the resentment of the working class. Workers wanted a say in where capital investments would be made, especially since investment at home meant new factories and more jobs for them. They objected to colonial wars in defense of these investments, such as Britain's Boer War (1899–1902) in South Africa, which could cost them their lives as well as their livelihood. The workers did not have to sit by idly and watch colonialism spread. At least they could participate in the political process and express their dissatisfaction.

Conditions had improved, and as Marx himself had seen, many workers were actively involved within the capitalist system, seeking to voice their discontents and to improve the quality of their lives. During Marx's lifetime, with the establishment of the Third French Republic in 1875, all French males could vote for the lower house of the French legislature. Marx was also aware that in a unified Germany, by 1871 all adult males could vote for members of the lower house of the legislature, even though the powers of the lower house were in fact quite limited. In England, by 1884 the right to vote for members of Parliament was extended to include all males except those who lived with their parents or were employed as live-in domestic servants or farmhands.

By 1884, labor unions had obtained legal recognition in France. While craft unions, composed of members of the same skilled trades, had been established in Great Britain as early as the 1850s, by the turn of the century, industrial unions, composed of unskilled workers, also began to form. The German Empire, too, had accepted the right of unions to exist. In 1900, there were about two million union members in Great Britain, 850,000 in Germany, and 250,000 in France.

By the late 1880s workers' political parties were represented in the national legislatures of France and Germany. In France, workers were a relatively small segment of the population. The political system was very fragmented with many small parties competing with one another for votes. The most prominent French party to voice an interest in the workers was the Radical Socialists, but the workers were to be disappointed with this party's representatives. As they soon found out, the party was more concerned with the needs of small shopkeepers and peasants than with labor's problems. Radical Socialists even took steps to put down strikes and slow the process of unionization.

The German Social Democratic Party, a Marxist organization, was founded in 1875 in Gotha. Marx himself had criticized the party's platform. He had objected to a number of specific proposals, such as state control of public education. What troubled him most was the platform's failure to address itself to the future, to the coming of a communist society. He was especially critical of Ferdinand Lassalle his former friend and one of the party's founders. However, Marx always targeted former friends for scorn when they strayed from, misinterpreted, or neglected his doctrines. From 1878 to 1890, the German government, led by conservative Count Otto von Bismarck, banned socialist organizations and publications. They went underground. However, socialist legislators continued to be elected to serve in office; the party polled 493,000 votes in 1877, 1,427,000 votes in 1890, and 4,239,000 votes by 1912. Banning the party did not prevent voters from supporting it, and by the 1890s the antisocialist laws were abandoned.

In England, by the turn of the century, the Labour Party had been formed and sent members to Parliament. Working-class representatives had sat with Liberal members of Parliament since 1885. English trade unions had been so successful in satisfying workers' demands that the need for separate political representation developed more slowly.

Unionism and the rise of workers' political parties in France and Germany had been impeded by the legacy of fear and distrust left over from the bitter destruction and fighting that brought an end to the Paris Commune in 1871. Yet the governments did not ignore the need for social legislation and, in the case of Germany, sometimes used it to lure workers from their socialist loyalties. In Germany in the 1880s, the government enacted a broad program of social legislation insuring workers against sickness, accident, and old age. Bismarck was trying to counteract the appeal of socialist movements by co-opting some of their proposals. The legislation was even extended after 1890 when he was forced to resign from office. In France between 1890 and 1910, some social legislation was passed to improve the lot of the workers. In Great Britain, from 1874 to 1880, regulations concerning factory and mine conditions were broadened and extended. Then from 1906 to 1916, the British Parliament passed a fairly comprehensive social insurance program, including old-age, accident, and sickness insurance, some measure of unemployment insurance as well as a minimum wage law.

Circumstances in the industrialized nations of western Europe had indeed changed. Had he lived longer, Marx himself might have argued that the change in objective conditions required changes in subjective conditions. In other words, he might have felt himself required to adjust his theories to new realities. In the latter part of his life, he did acknowledge the benefits the British trade unions had achieved for their members. He did urge workers to enter politics to achieve at least their short-term goals. On the other hand, he never ceased to regard himself as a revolutionary. What Marx would have done is unknown. This is an issue that can never be resolved. What Marx's successors did do is well documented. It is their differing views that created divisions within the Marxist movement from the time of Marx's death until the outbreak of World War I.

Not only did his disciples continue to defend Marxist theories from rival socialist formulations, they also had to apply Marxist doctrines to a changing set of circumstances and that caused them to disagree among themselves as to what Marx actually said. As long as Engels lived, there was at least one source of authority to whom they could turn for guidance, but Engels died in 1895. The problems of interpretation while Engels lived grew even more complicated upon his death.

All of the changes and improvements in working-class life had affected the popularity of Marxism in the industrialized countries of western Europe. In England, Marxism was unable to compete with Fabian Socialism, which preached gradual change through social reform. In France, the working-class movement was small and not powerful. Although Marxism wasn't abandoned after the failure of the Paris Commune, it was treated with a certain degree of suspicion. Those who might have been Marxists preached anarchism, a doctrine of violent radical protests against all forms of authority, instead. However, when anarchism lost its grip on French socialist thought, it was replaced by syndicalism. This school of thought advocated that workers go out on a general strike to bring down all economic and political institutions. These were to be replaced by syndicates, organizations composed of and controlled by workers.

It was mainly in central Europe, particularly Germany, where the Marxist Social Democratic party kept growing in strength, that socialists addressed themselves to the Marxist legacy. However, their difficulties were illustrative of the problems faced by Marxists in other countries as well. They faced the problems of squaring Marxist doctrines with the vast improvement in workers' lives and with workers' increased political activity.

How they should interpret Marx's varied doctrines and theories became the subject of intense debate. Since it appeared that a number of Marx's predictions were not coming true, should they continue to preserve his theories just as he presented them, or should they modify the theories and reinterpret them? How should they handle the ambiguities they found in Marx's writings?

Anyone who subscribes to a particular set of beliefs that attempts to explain the way things are and to predict the way they will be persistently faces these problems. The way things are tends to change over time, but not necessarily in the way that was predicted. If the beliefs and predictions are not adapted to the changes, they can easily become outmoded and invalid. On the other hand, if they are interpreted to take the changes into account, they may become internally inconsistent and contradictory, or they may be made broad and general. If the beliefs are very broad and vague in content, they can be more easily adjusted to changing times. However, if they are too broad, too vague, they may be useless as practical guides to change. They risk becoming meaningless, empty, commonplace statements, or platitudes.

Marx's central European successors faced all these difficulties. Would capitalism inevitably fall? Was the concept of the class struggle still valid? Was a proletarian revolution still necessary to bring about socialism? Was a communist utopia attainable? Their attempts to resolve these issues and others gave rise to a variety of interpretations of Marx's ideas and eventually to competing factions within the socialist movement. Between 1890 and 1910, a period of prosperity and economic expansion, differences arose between what became known as the Orthodox Marxists and the Revisionists.

A principal spokesman for the Orthodox, or traditional, mainstream Marxists was Karl Kautsky (1854–1938). In 1883, the year of Marx's death, he became the editor of *Neue Zeit (New Times)*, a German Social Democratic party publication. Kautsky treated dialectical materialism as a form of evolutionary development. He tended to emphasize Marx's economic arguments rather than his more revolutionary or utopian proposals, so he focused on the increasing misery of the proletariat and the further consolidation of industries. He expected the inevitable decline of capitalism. Kautsky retained the concept of class struggle by rejecting compromise with the bourgeois state and the possibility of an alliance with peasants to bring about change. Also he believed that workers could gain control of the state through peaceful means, by working within the system. In effect, he abandoned the idea of a violent proletarian revolution. His belief in peaceful means extended to international relations, where he refused to support wars or violence.

Eduard Bernstein (1850–1932) believed that it was necessary to adjust Marxist doctrines to the changing realities of the proletariat. He emerged as a founding father of revisionism. Revisionists saw socialism as a reformist movement exerting economic pressure to achieve its goals. They abandoned all ideas of revolution and the proletarian dictatorship in favor of an evolutionary approach to change. Bernstein regarded economic determinism and dialectical materialism as unscientific and too simplistic. Marxist economics, such as the theory of surplus value, were discarded as obsolete. Bernstein even argued that capitalist crises would become less frequent as industries consolidated. Class warfare was replaced by the idea of cooperation with the bourgeoisie.

Moreover, since the workers were no longer outsiders, they, too, would have nationalist loyalties. He rejected Marx's vision of a communist society as utopian and replaced it with a broader conception of democracy.

Karl Kautsky and others quickly came to the defense of what they claimed to be the orthodox interpretation of Marxism. They continued to believe in the inevitability of a proletarian revolution, but whereas Marx expected the proletariat to overthrow the state, the Orthodox Marxists expected them to control it. Unlike the Revisionists, they continued to insist that the capitalist system would fall as Marx had predicted because they still believed that his theories were scientifically valid. They used Marxist revolutionary phrases as a means of frightening the bourgeoisie into yielding to proletarian demands, but their methods were quite peaceful. Practically speaking, there was little difference between the Revisionists and the Orthodox Marxists in the techniques they used. However, the Orthodox Marxists still paid lip service to Marx's revolutionary rhetoric, whereas the Revisionists were more willing to concede openly that Marx's views were becoming outdated. Both deplored the use of violence to obtain workers' objectives. Orthodox Marxists held that the class struggle would continue, but in a democratic context.

Orthodox Marxists were confronted with new challenges as Europe drew nearer to the eve of World War I. A radical movement within the German Social Democratic party emerged that was critical of the democratic and legal methods practiced by both the Orthodox Marxists and the Revisionists. Rosa Luxemburg (1870–1919) was one of the prominent radical leaders who was dissatisfied with the reformist mentality of the Marxists of her day. For Luxemburg, Marx's scientific method was still valid and thus his predictions. However, Luxemburg extended Marx's arguments so that they applied to a broader arena. She grafted onto Marxism a theory of imperialism. She recognized that the major industrial states of Europe were competing for colonies. She interpreted this development solely in economic terms, arguing that capitalist systems constantly needed new markets because that was the only way they could increase their profits. Colonies provided the new markets. When capitalist expansion reached its limit, when there were no more colonies to exploit, capitalism would collapse and the proletarian revolution could take place.

For Luxemburg, the concept of class struggle was still valid. She still believed that the proletariat was a force outside the existing society with no ties other than those of class. She sought to realize Marx's goal of a communist society. She wanted workers to use the general strike to shut down all production and services within an area and to revolt when possible. Even if these actions failed, they would serve a purpose. They would prepare workers for an eventual proletarian revolution. Thus she advocated the use of violence. She insisted that a capitalist crisis would arise shortly and that the proletariat should be ready to seize power. Its revolution would be a spontaneous uprising. The workers, not their intellectual leaders and sympathizers, would take charge.

The men and women who dedicated their lives to preserving and interpreting Marxist theory were not isolated, unknown, aspiring socialists. For the most part, they were members of party organizations and participated in the Second International, a loose federation of socialist groups that held congresses every three years in different European cities. In 1889, representatives of the socialist parties and trade unions had met in Paris to form the Second International. It was regarded as the highest moral authority in the socialist movement. The source of that authority was Marxism. During the First International, Marxism was one of several competing socialist doctrines, but now it had achieved primacy of a sort. This is why, in 1896, the International expelled anarchist members. They were not prepared to accept authority of any kind, whether that of democracy or of the much interpreted Marxism of the era.

The International supported parliamentary democracy. Yet it did not believe that socialism could be achieved by means of cooperation with bourgeois parties. The International reaffirmed the Marxist doctrine of the class struggle and the inevitability of a proletarian revolution. What was most important to its members was the prevention of war, so it drafted many proposals for such schemes as courts of arbitration to settle international disputes and arms reduction.

By the outbreak of World War I, the socialist movement was split into factions, each moving in different directions. The British, the French, and the Russians fought against the Germans and the Austrians. International bonds uniting workers against nationalistic capitalist governments never materialized as workers took to the factories and the battlefields. The Second International dissolved. It looked as though Marxism would fast become an obsolete set of ideas, worthy only of study in textbooks on the history of Western civilization.

Then as World War I was raging on the battlefields of Europe, a revolution toppled the Czarist regime in Russia in March 1917. Russia was a vast, backward nation that Marx himself had dismissed as too primitive to have a socialist revolution. His European successors shared his views of this autocratic empire. Yet, in November 1917, to the surprise of these European Marxists, as well as the rest of the world, a group of dedicated Russian Marxists, who called themselves Bolsheviks, seized power from the new government of Russia and set about establishing a Marxist regime. Determined to succeed, they began to give Marxism a new set of meanings and interpretations. Like the proverbial phoenix, Marxism rose from the ashes of World War I.

The man most responsible for the success of the

Marxist revolution in Russia was Vladimir Ilyich Lenin (1870–1924). He turned Marxism from a set of doctrines debated by European socialists into a dynamic revolutionary force, a force that could actually overthrow governments. Not only did he breathe new life into Marxist ideas, he put them into practice, something no other Marxist had been able to do. In Lenin's hands, Marxism became a set of beliefs and practices for ruling peoples as well as for conducting successful revolutions. It became the ideology of the powerful as well as the powerless. Lenin gave Marxism the form familiar to people today.

To adapt Marx's ideas to a backward nation like Russia as well as to nations fighting World War I, Lenin had to make a number of adjustments in traditional Marxist thinking. He altered accepted views on the nature of the class struggle, the nature of the revolution, the role of the Marxist party, the aftermath of revolution, and the international relationships of capitalist powers.

Orthodox Marxists, revisionists, and radicals in Europe concentrated on defining the workers' role in the class struggle, but Lenin recognized that in Russia, the working classes were but a very small percentage of the population. He understood that no revolution would succeed if it limited its appeal solely to this tiny proletarian class. For this reason, he began to pay attention to the poorer peasantry, those who would be regarded as agricultural laborers or small farmers today. He stressed the common interests of the workers and peasants to urge them on to revolution and no longer regarded the workers as the only revolutionary class in society. Lenin insisted that the class struggle would be fought by proletarians and poor peasants against bourgeois landowners as well as factory owners. This is the combination of classes that has managed to wage most of the successful Marxist revolutions of the twentieth century. But, then, most modern Marxist revolutions have occurred in underdeveloped countries such as Russia was in 1917.

Lenin also transformed the nature of Marxist revolution. Marx had anticipated that a revolution would break out spontaneously; Lenin disagreed. He reasoned that workers would be concerned only with improving their conditions of employment and increasing their wages. He did not believe they would ever become revolutionaries on their own. Instead, he maintained that Marxist parties, not the workers, would have to decide when and where to act. Spontaneity would be replaced with planning and controls. The revolutionary leadership would deliberately use incidents and events to rouse people to overturn their governments. The people would fight to bring the revolutionary leadership to power over them. They would not be fighting to gain power themselves. In fact, today, Marxist spontaneity has been replaced by Leninist planning and Lenin-style leadership.

In Lenin's day, most Social Democratic (Marxist) parties were loose associations of members led by elected officials that offered candidates for election and debated issues openly. Lenin felt that in a repressive society like Russia, such open, democratic meetings were doomed to failure. They could too easily be penetrated by agents of the existing authorities. Their plans could too readily be discovered by the governments they were trying to bring down. Governments could also ban parties they felt were threats to their power. For parties to provide revolutionary leadership, Lenin argued, they would have to become highly disciplined, secretive, and centralized. The party Lenin visualized and later organized was very similar to an underground movement.

Its leadership was to be centralized in a very small group of experienced, like-minded revolutionaries who would make all the important decisions for the Marxist movement. The party membership, also small in number, would have the self-control, or discipline, to accept the decisions of the leadership without question. The party organization resembled a pyramid with the membership forming a base. These members would elect a central committee to represent them, and the central committee, in turn, would elect the leadership. All decisions would flow downward from the top of the pyramid. Lenin called this democratic centralism because the leadership was elected, albeit indirectly. Thus democracy was practiced, but decisions were made and controlled by the top, hence the command of the party was centralized.

Lenin regarded this party as the vanguard of the proletariat, the term Marx had used to describe those who understood and sought to realize the historic mission of the proletariat. Marx had never wanted the vanguard to be confined to a self-perpetuating group of individuals, to an elite; nor had he expected it to determine or even dictate revolutionary policy. He had wanted this group to cooperate with workers' parties and coordinate their efforts to bring about revolution. However, Lenin's interpretation is the one that has become the model for revolutionary societies today.

Marx had vaguely described the immediate postrevolutionary government as a dictatorship of the proletariat whose function it was to swiftly bring about a true communist society. Lenin retained Marx's term, but it soon became clear that the elitist party he had built to bring about a Marxist revolution would stay in power to govern as the dictatorship of the proletariat. Not only would it serve to eliminate traces of bourgeois society as Marx expected, but it would continue to rule in order to protect the Marxist revolution from its enemies abroad. Marx had not anticipated this need. From Lenin's standpoint, the party-controlled government was also vital to direct and manage the industrialization of the economy. Marx, of course, had assumed that industrialization would have already taken place. Communists today often justify the continuance of their government by claiming that while they have achieved socialism, they have yet to attain a true communist state of perfect equality and sharing as envisaged by Marx. So Marxism has become a system of government-imposed conformity instead of the creative, spontaneous, cooperative society that Marx had promised.

To describe relationships among capitalist powers, Lenin set forth his own doctrine of imperialism, building upon the works of others. His interpretation has become the official doctrine of the communist movement. In a series of arguments similar to Rosa Luxemburg's, Lenin maintained that the major European powers, under the domination of a few powerful banks, had scrambled for colonies to enable the banks to achieve greater profits. Rivalries among nations intensified because some countries controlled more colonies than others. Coalitions of nations formed to support or oppose the redistribution of colonies, and according to Lenin, it was over this issue that World War I erupted. He insisted that imperialism would inevitably lead to war among rival capitalist states. He reasoned that as long as capitalist systems existed, imperialism would continue, since capitalists needed colonies in order to increase their profits.

To explain why some socialists supported the war effort, Lenin distinguished between better-paid workers and underpaid workers. The better-paid workers, among whom Lenin placed trade union and socialist party leaders, benefited from their countries' colonial possessions in the form of higher wages. This is why they were willing to support the war. The underpaid workers opposed the war because they had nothing to gain from it.

As a result of Lenin's revisions of Marxism, the theory that Marx had written was transformed to appeal to people in backward, underdeveloped nations, to justify the government of the few over the many. As was shown, the phrases Marx used were still kept, but the meanings were altered. For example, "proletarian revolution" became the revolution of workers and peasants. "Dictatorship of the proletariat" became rule by the Communist party, whose membership was limited to an exclusive few. In this new guise, Marxism became a potent force in the twentieth century.

FURTHER READING

Evans, Michael. *Karl Marx.* Bloomington: Indiana University Press, 1975.

Feuer, Lewis S. *Marx and Engels: Basic Writings on Politics and Philosophy.* New York: Anchor Books, 1959.

Lichtheim, George. *Marxism: An Historical and Critical Study.* New York: Frederick A. Praeger, 1961.

Marx, Karl and Friedrich Engels. *The Communist Manifesto.* Joseph Katz, ed. New York: Pocket Books, 1964.

McLellan, David. *Marx Before Marxism.* 2d ed. London: Macmillan, 1980.

Meyer, Alfred G. *Marxism: The Unity of Theory and Practice.* Ann Arbor: Univ. of Michigan Press, 1963.

Padover, Saul K. *Karl Marx: An Intimate Biography.* New York: McGraw-Hill, 1978.

Savage, Katherine. *The Story of Marxism and Communism.* New York: Walck, 1968.

Tucker, Robert, ed. *The Marx-Engels Reader.* New York: W. W. Norton, 1972.

INDEX

Agoult, Countess d', 23, 25
Anneke, Friedrich, 41
Annenkov, Pavel, 31
Austria, 35-36

Bakunin, Mikhail, 24, 55-56
Bauer, Bruno, 16-18, 75
Belgium, 27-31, 37-38
Bernstein, Eduard, 111
Bismarck, Count Otto von, 37, 107-108
Blanc, Louis, 39
Boer War, 106
Bolsheviks, 114
Bonaparte, Louis-Napoleon, 35, 45, 54
Bourgeoisie, 73, 77-78, 80-81, 84, 89, 98-99
Brussels, Belgium, Marx in, 27-31, 37-38
Burns, Mary, 50

Capital, 3, 54, 80, 84
Capitalism, 73, 76-77, 79-80, 84-85
Civil War in France, The, 56
Class struggle, 67-69, 72, 85, 90

Cologne, Germany, Marx in, 40-44, 85
Commune, defined, 99
Communism, 1-2, 26, 94-99, 117
Communist League, 30-32, 38-40, 49, 54
Communist Manifesto, 3, 32-33, 38, 97-98
Contribution to the Critique of Political Economy, A, 54
Critique of the Gotha Program, 57

Dana, Charles, 52
Darwin, Charles, 74
Delmuth, Helene ("Lenchen"), 28, 44-45, 50-51, 57
Democracy, Western, defined, 1-2
Deutsche-Brusseler-Zeitung (*German-Belgian Times*), 30
Deutsche-Franzosische Jahrbucher (*German-French Yearbook*), 22
Dialectical materialism, 62-68, 80, 83, 104

Economics, in Marxist theory, 65-66, 67-70, 74, 76-77, 92

■120■

Eighteenth Brumaire of Louis Bonaparte, The, 45, 54
Engels, Friedrich, 3, 25–26, 29–33, 38–42, 44–46, 48, 50–54, 56–57, 84, 99, 103–104, 109
England, 47–48, 52, 54, 91, 105–109

Fabian Socialism, 109
Family, in Marxist theory, 66, 73, 95
Feuerbach, Ludwig, 29, 64
First International (International Workingmen's Association), 54–56, 88, 113
Fourier, Charles, 103
France, 19, 22, 27, 34–35, 37–38, 45–46, 69, 90–91, 105–109
Franco-Prussian War, 56, 91
Frederick William III, King of Prussia, 12
Frederick William IV, King of Prussia, 18, 20, 27, 36–37

German Ideology, The, 29–30
German Workers' Education Society, 29–30
Germany, 3, 9, 11, 14, 36, 40–42, 53, 91, 106–108, 110
Gottschalk, Andreas, 40–41
Greeley, Horace, 52
Guizot, François, 22, 27

Hapsburgs of Austria, 35–36
Hegel, Georg, 16, 63–64, 66
Heine, Heinrich, 25, 38
Herr Vogt, 54
Herwegh, Georg, 24, 38–41
Hess, Moses, 31
History, in Marxist theory, 61–71, 90

Industrial Revolution, 47–48, 86, 89
Iron law of wages, 72

Kautsky, Karl, 111–112
Kriege, Hermann, 31

Labor theory of value, 76–78

Labor unions, 55, 81, 89, 106–108
LaFargue, Paul, 57
Lassalle, Ferdinand, 53, 55, 107
League of the Just, 29, 32
Lenin, Vladimir Ilyich, 92–93, 115–118
Leopold I, King of Belgium, 28
Liebknecht, Wilhelm, 50
Lissagaray, Hippolyte Prosper-Olivier, 57
Locke, John, 76
London, England, Marx in, 29, 32, 46–50, 52–54, 57, 73
Longuet, Charles, 57
Louis-Philippe, King of France, 22, 27, 34–35
Luxemburg, Rosa, 112–113, 118

Marx, Edgar, 32, 51
Marx, Edmund Heinrich ("Guido"), 49–51
Marx, Eleanor, 52–53, 57
Marx, Francesca, 51
Marx, Heinrich, 10–12, 14–15
Marx, Jenny, 25, 53
Marx, Jenny von Westphalen, 20–23, 27–29, 32, 37–38, 44–45, 49–51, 53, 57
Marx, Karl
　arrests, 37, 43–44
　birth and childhood, 10–11
　children, 25, 27, 29, 32, 49–53, 57
　death, 57
　education, 11–18
　marriage, 21
Marx, Laura, 29, 50, 53, 57
Marxism, changes in, 1, 111–118
Marxist nations, 2, 69–70, 114–118
Metternich, Count, 9

Neue Rheinische Zeitung (*New Rhine Times*), 40–41, 52, 55
New York Tribune, The, 52
Nicaragua, 69–70

Owen, Robert, 103
Orthodox Marxism, 111–112, 115

■121■

Paris, France, Marx in, 22–23, 25–27, 38–39, 45
Paris Commune, 56–57, 91, 108–109
Peasants, 4, 115
Philips, Lion, 51
Poverty of Philosophy, The, 31
Private enterprise, defined, 1–2
Proletariat, in Marxist theory, 73, 82–83. *See also* Workers.
Proudhon, Pierre Joseph, 24, 31–32, 55
Prussia, 9, 22, 27, 30, 36–37, 40, 43, 105

Raw communism. *See* Communism
Religion, in Marxist theory, 17, 61, 74–75, 81
Revisionist marxism, 111–112, 115
Revolution, in Marxist theory, 85–88, 90–91, 93
Revolutions of 1848, in Europe, 46, 85, 91
Rheinische Zeitung (*Rhine Times*), 19–20, 22, 25
Ruge, Arnold, 22, 24–25
Russia, 6, 20, 56, 87, 93, 114–116
Russian Revolution, 6, 90–91, 114–118
Rutenberg, Adolf, 19

Saint-Simon, Henri de, 103

Schurz, Carl, 41
Second French Republic, 35, 45
Second International, 113–114
Social Darwinism, 74
Socialism, 23–24, 26, 54, 103–104, 107, 109–111
State, the, in Marxist theory, 98–100, 117–118
Surplus value, theory of, 77–78, 111
Soviets, 6, 117–118

Theses on Feuerbach, 29
Third French Republic, 106
Trier, Prussia, Marx in, 11, 29, 40, 53

Victoria, Queen of England, 47
Vorwarts (*Forward*), 25, 27

Weitlung, Wilhelm, 31
Wilhelm I, King of Prussia, 53
Willich, August von, 49
Wolff, Wilhelm, 53
Workers, in Marxist theory, 68, 71–78, 81–83, 91
World War I, 6, 88, 109, 112, 114–115, 118
World War II, 88

Young Hegelians (club), 15–19, 23, 26, 33

JUL -- 2011